Quiet Moments for Nurses

Quiet Moments for Nurses

Biblical Reflections for Rest and Renewal

Second Edition

Sharon Fish Mooney

RESOURCE *Publications* • Eugene, Oregon

QUIET MOMENTS FOR NURSES
Biblical Reflections for Rest and Renewal

Resource Publications
An imprint of Wipf and Stock Publishers
199 W. 8th Ave., Suite 3
Eugene, OR 97401
www. wipfandstock.com

PAPERBACK ISBN: 979-8-3852-7775-9
HARDCOVER ISBN: 979-8-3852-7776-6
EBOOK ISBN: 979-8-3852-7777-3

Originally published by Vine Books, an imprint of Servant Publications. 2000.
Also distributed by Regal Books, a Division of Gospel Light.

To protect the privacy of individuals whose stories are told in this book, names have been fictionalized. With permission, real names are portrayed in some of the devotionals.

I dedicate this book to
Dorothy Oswald,
who exemplifies nursing at its finest.

Contents

Amazing Grace

Foreword

We nurses live fast-paced lives, filled with responsibilities and demands that often drain us. We need an oasis of peace along our journey—regular times to hear God speaking into the frenzy of our minds and hearts.

Quiet Moments for Nurses provides nurture and refreshment, bringing God's perspective into the realities of nursing. Author Sharon Fish Mooney walks in our shoes. She has worked in acute and long-term care, in community heath and nursing education. She knows the challenges of graduate school as well as a wide spectrum of nursing practice. Sharon has also experienced the fulfillment and frustration of caring for her mother with Alzheimer's disease.

Enjoy the treasures Sharon has prepared for nurses and nursing students. Savor the thought-provoking essays that weave Scripture into our lives. This book is a gold mine of inspiration.

As you use the book, the table of contents can help you assess your own needs and decide where to begin. After you reflect on Sharon's example of meditating on Scripture, consider reading the surrounding verses in your own Bible. Continue to mine the treasures from God.

As well as being a gift to individual nurses, *Quiet Moments for Nurses* is a resource for nurses and nursing students who meet in small groups. Sharon's focused and insightful Scripture-based messages will be a rich foundation for discussion and prayer. Plan some refreshment breaks with *Quiet Moments for Nurses* over lunch, before work or classes. Read a chapter, discuss application in your own nursing situation and talk with Jesus together.

This book encouraged me to celebrate how God enters our world of nursing. May you and your friends be inspired in the same way. God is with us in all our nursing roles. Anticipate the Lord's blessing in your nursing practice as you learn from *Quiet Moments for Nurses.*

Mary Thompson, RN, MSN (1939–2023)
Director, Nurses Christian Fellowship USA (1984–2007)
Madison, Wisconsin

Strength
for the Journey

Strength for the Journey

> *...but they who wait for the Lord shall renew their strength, they shall mount up with wings like eagles, they shall run and not be weary, they shall walk and not faint.*
>
> Isaiah 40:31

I was a brand-new graduate nurse and it was my first apartment. My parents were not impressed. There were cockroaches in the kitchen and rats in the basement. But it was mine and it was cheap.

The route I needed to take to get to my car each night to go to work led me through the apartment complex basement. It was a dark, dank place that impressed my parents even less than the roaches and rodents, and, in fact, was probably their breeding ground.

My routine, most nights I worked, was the same. I'd get in my car, turn on the overhead light and read either a Psalm or some verses from Isaiah before heading for the hospital. Strength for the journey, I called it.

That first year as a new grad was a year of learning new skills, testing my wings, making mistakes. I didn't feel very mighty or strong. *Weak* and *klutzy* were more apt descriptions. It was also a year that gave me a new appreciation of the meaning of the phrase "waiting for the Lord." Isaiah 40:31 became my theme verse.

Before I became a nurse, the concept that I most associated with waiting was patience—of my needing to be patient when God's answer seemed to be *no.* Now I know that phrase has a flip side. Strength for the journey comes not in my waiting for the Lord to do something for me, but in my waiting for the Lord to do something for him. A person who waits for the Lord serves the Lord. One image that comes to mind when

I read Isaiah 40:31 is that of a servant waiting for or waiting on a king or queen or some other person in authority. But I also envision a nurse, waiting patiently for or waiting patiently on people in need. This may mean gently and patiently washing the feet of a homeless man in the ER. It may mean waiting patiently with attentiveness for an elder in a nursing home to share his or her life story with you for the fifth time that morning. It may mean waiting patiently and with encouragement for a sick child on the pediatric unit to take his medicine.

Isaiah tells me my strength comes by waiting as I lovingly and patiently serve the people God created in his image and for his glory. Lord, renew my strength today and teach me to patiently wait—for you.

The Promise Box

> *For all the promises of God find their Yes in him. That is why we utter the Amen through him, to the glory of God.*
>
> 2 Corinthians 1:20

Initially I visited Leonhard Laton for a nursing course I was taking on qualitative research. I needed an "old, old Christian" to interview. At age eighty-nine, Mr. Laton was the perfect choice. After the course I found myself going back to visit just because I enjoyed visiting.

At the end of each visit we would pray—not a short and simple prayer but long prayers on our knees. It took a little time for Mr. Laton to get down on his knees, because of his arthritis, but once down I was very glad he made the effort. It was evident Mr. Laton was intimately acquainted with God, and my need was to simply learn from him. One day he told me that prayer was "like breathing. Your heart gets full and you overbubble. That's how you talk to God." So Mr. Laton would overbubble, and I would simply listen and enjoy.

When prayer was ended I'd help Mr. Laton to his feet. Then he'd put the kettle on, and we'd have a cup of tea. After tea he would reach into the cardboard shoebox he kept at the corner of his kitchen table and pull out several five-by-eight cards and hand them to me. "These will help you in your times of crisis," he'd always say. There were well over two hundred cards in Mr. Laton's shoebox. Verses of Scripture were carefully handwritten on each card in various colors of ink. Many, he said, were "promises from God" that he wrote to "edify myself" and "give me strength." He told me that his life was "very rich" and that even though he was alone he had "no loneliness" because he had "the Word of God" that he was "printing and reading always."

I'd take those cards home each time I visited and stick them in my Bible. Some have become my bookmarks, verses from a "promise box" of someone who has walked with God for a very long time, much longer than I, much closer.

Someday, perhaps, I'll make my own promise box with verses God has given me, penned in different colors of ink. Someday, too, perhaps a nurse taking a research course will want to come and visit me when I'm an old, old Christian. I hope if the nurse does, I'll have learned the meaning of overbubbling in prayerful response to the God who gives me promises.

Bentoverness

> *And when Jesus saw her, he called her and said to her "Woman, you are freed from your infirmity."*
>
> Luke 13:12

Whenever they touched her she would cry out in pain. It soon became apparent that getting Mrs. Ryan dressed in the morning was not going to be an easy task for the nursing assistants, or a pleasant one for Mrs. Ryan.

Soon the physician was notified, and pain medication was ordered to be given a half hour before the dressing attempt; this did not completely eliminate the pain, but it considerably alleviated it.

Mrs. Ryan suffered from osteoporosis and severe arthritis. When standing, her body bent over at a ninety-degree angle, with fragile arms locked tightly against her chest.

Caring for people with chronic bone and joint disease is never an easy task. As nurses we need to anticipate the pain that comes from engaging in even routine activities of daily living. We look for ways to alleviate that pain with traditional treatments like medication, heat and massage. We can also pray that the medications and treatments will be effective.

Jesus recognized the pain of bentoverness and took the initiative to alleviate it. Luke tells the story of a woman who had suffered from a spirit of infirmity for eighteen years; we don't know specifically what she suffered from, but whatever it was it caused her to be bent over, unable to fully straighten herself (Luke 13:10–17).

This woman appears to be a woman of faith. Jesus was in the synagogue on the Sabbath, and the woman might have been listening to him teach. I picture her trying to get close to him, shuffling forward perhaps with a walker or a cane.

Suddenly Jesus stopped teaching and looked up. Perhaps he heard her cry of pain or, more likely, sensed it. He called to her, out of the crowd gathered around him. "Woman," he said, "you are freed from your infirmity." Then he went one step further: he laid his hands on her bentoverness and made her straight.

As nurses we can also suffer from our own versions of bentoverness and pain associated with our own infirmities—spiritual, emotional and physical. Put yourself in this woman's place today. What causes you to be bent over, unable to live your life fully because of some infirmity from the past? It may be a physical ailment but more likely it's a spiritual or emotional disability Jesus needs to set you free from. Perhaps it's a long-standing problem accompanied by guilt or shame, the two things that cause us to *stay* bentover, unable to admit our need and receive the help we need for overcoming.

Come to Jesus today and let him free you completely from whatever it is in your past that causes pain in your present. If you are free yourself, perhaps you know someone at home or at work who is bound by some infirmity and needs a healing touch. Bring them to Jesus in your prayers this morning.

Be Still and Know

> *Be still, and know that I am God. I am exalted among the nations, I am exalted in the earth!*
>
> Psalm 46:10

Nurses are rarely still. For eight-hour and twelve-hour shifts and often for the sixteen-hour "double" we are constantly in motion. Ellen, a new graduate friend of mine who works on an orthopedic unit, clocked five miles one day on the pedometer her jogger husband loaned her. Yet God tells us to be still. It is not a suggestion, but a command.

"But how?" you ask. "I'm overworked, my unit is understaffed, and I'm surrounded by accidents waiting to happen. Visions of lawsuits dance in my head. Be still? Are you kidding? Just consider my circumstances!"

Circumstances were also important to the Sons of Korah, who lived in tough and troubled times. These sacred musicians wrote Psalm 46 for their choirmaster, who, like us, may have faced not a few problems at work. The earth could change and the mountains might shake in the heart of the sea, his singers tell him (v. 2). The waters might roar and foam (v. 3).

As nurses, we can identify with those not-good days. I remember times in nursing when my own heart shook a bit and trembled: medication errors, code blues, nursing boards! It's easy, too, to identify with the roaring and foaming. It might be the loss of a job that threatens to pull us under financially.

"The nations rage, the kingdoms totter," sang the Sons of Korah (v. 6). Patients and their friends and relatives may get angry with you, testing your ability to keep your cool and respond with grace. Or perhaps it's a nursing management that seems unresponsive to your needs and those of your coworkers. There's also your home situation and your family in crisis—death, divorce, disease, disaster. Your world tilts.

The command to "be still" came to people in the midst of turmoil, just as it comes to us. The Sons of Korah list the reasons why we can be still. Their most important one is God, our refuge and our strength; God, our very present, well-proved help in time of trouble; God, with us.

It's not easy to be still "in the midst," but that is what we're called to be. Korah's sons tell us God is in the midst of the city, his holy habitation. "God is in the midst of her, she shall not be moved; God will help her right early" (v. 5).

We need to personalize the Psalms. *We* are God's holy habitation, his dwelling place. God is in *our* midst. *We* shall not be moved. He will help *us*—right early.

There are eleven other psalms of the Sons of Korah, and in all their songs their message is the same. God is "in our midst."

Being still is not a call to sit down, put your feet up and have a cup of coffee—a very pleasant thought in times of trouble. Being still is assurance of God's very present help in the midst of our daily chaos—in the midst of our raging, tilting, tottering worlds.

We need not fear.

Be still, and know that he is God.

Selah.

Bruised Reeds and Dimly Burning Wicks

> *...a bruised reed he will not break, and a dimly burning wick he will not quench; he will faithfully bring forth justice.*
>
> Isaiah 42:3

I remember the morning I broke my mother's cane.*

As director for a home care agency, responsibility weighed heavy on me that morning when the call came that my scheduler was ill. I needed to get to the office.

Morning routines for me usually consisted of getting my mother out of bed, bathing her, dressing her, feeding her, rushing off with her to an adult day-care center that specialized in caring for persons with dementia, and then heading for work. Mom had Alzheimer's disease and this was our usual morning routine. This particular morning, however, the routine changed.

When I tried to get Mom out of bed, she wrapped her arms around the side rail, yelling "No!" When I finally got her on her feet, she suddenly sat down on the rug. When I tried to get her up she began to strike my legs with her cane.

Mom didn't hit me hard, but I lost control. I grabbed her cane and banged it against the floor. Old and brittle, the cane snapped in two, lying broken beside my mother who was still sitting on the floor but now laughing.

I felt shame. I felt horror. I had so easily broken the cane in my anger and frustration. Would I ever be tempted to vent the same anger and frustration at my mother? Mom was still laughing and I remember laughing too. I sat down beside her on the floor and put my arms around her. Then I began to cry.

I finally made it to work, but the day itself was not a happy one, punctuated by memories of my morning. That night, after Mom was in bed, I sat down to spend some needed time with

God. The day's meditation was Isaiah 42, and my eyes landed on verse 3: "...a bruised reed he will not break, and a dimly burning wick he will not quench."

That bruised reed was my mother. Bruised reeds were also the other frail and elderly people I cared for each day in my job at the home-care agency, bruised in the battle against Alzheimer's and other chronic illnesses.

I was the dimly burning wick. My candle was flickering pretty badly that morning and I needed God's gentle reminder that he was not about to quench my smoldering wick and snuff me out but could help me deal with my anger in more appropriate ways.

Mom's candle was flickering too, and I began to get in touch with my feelings of both actual and impending loss, yet also with God's promise of continued, compassionate care for us both.

Nowhere, this side of eternity, has God promised to take us out of our world of suffering, loss and aggravations at home or at work that try our patience. But he has promised to walk through the suffering and loss with us, strengthening us in our weakness, disciplining our emotions, and fanning the flames of our flagging spirits.

*Adapted from Sharon Fish. *Alzheimer's: Caring for Your Loved One, Caring for Yourself.* (Harold Shaw Publishers, 1996).

Possessions

> *They shall have no inheritance; I am their inheritance: and you shall give them no possession in Israel; I am their possession.*
>
> Ezekiel 44:28

The boxes were piling up in the living room. I counted fifty. Soon they spilled over into the kitchen and finally the bathroom. This move to Canada was making me painfully aware of the fact I had way too much stuff. I found myself easily identifying with the young man in Matthew 19:22 who "went away sorrowful; for he had great possessions." But surely I might need this, I reasoned. This chair leg's broken but the chair is still serviceable. I just might teach pharmacology again in the future; I'd better save these notes and books. Do I really need three crock pots? Well, I'll be teaching; maybe they'll come in handy if the students come over for a picnic. These boots I've only worn once. They hurt my feet a bit, but maybe they'll stretch with wear.

Possessions can become obsessions!

God's perspective on possessions is far different. Often, in Scripture, possessions are associated with the land, a good land, a place to dwell in. But possessions are also associated with God's people. The Israelites were called the "sons of the Lord." God had chosen them "to be a people for his own possession" (Deuteronomy 14:1–2). They were to be a people holy to the Lord, keeping his commandments (Deuteronomy 26:19). Christians, too, are sons and daughters of the Lord, chosen to be a people for his own possession, to be a people holy to the Lord and obedient to his Word.

Possessions are also associated with our future hope as Christians, that imperishable, undefiled and unfading inheritance of which our present-day relationship with Christ on earth is but the "first installment."

The priests of Israel in the days of the prophet Ezekiel were reminded of what their true inheritance was. It did not consist of land or other material goods. Their possession was to be God himself. As a member of that royal and holy priesthood today (1 Peter 2:5), I, too, can say "God is my possession." I realize I need to say it more, especially in the midst of packing.

Do I really need this book, this pot, this piece of furniture? Am I clinging to it just because of sentimental value? Is it weighing me down or freeing me to serve God better? Would it be worth more to someone else than to me if I gave it away or sold it? I'm reminded that the young man in Matthew's gospel was told by Jesus to be obedient, sell at least some of his possessions and give to the poor.

Lord, today as I pack yet another box, let me focus my primary attention on you. Help me to cope with the clutter of my life and put it in perspective. Free me, not just from stuff, but from obsession with possessions. And help me be obsessed with one thing only. You.

Keep Your Head Down

> *Let your eyes look directly forward, and your gaze be straight before you.*
>
> Proverbs 4:25

Don't look up. Just keep your head down" was my father's favorite phrase and one he frequently needed to use with me on our weekly trips to the local golf course.

Golf, for me, is the ultimate sport and one that's a needed stress reliever on days or evenings off from nursing duties. My mother and father were weekend golfers and always dragged me along with them when I was a kid, rather than hire a sitter. I continued to golf through high school and college and later in life, when my mother developed Alzheimer's disease and my father and I were full-time caregivers, we'd hire home health care aides once a week and plan our own respite time around a morning at the golf course.

I had a tendency, though, and still do, to want to look up when I hit the ball to see where it's going. This tendency to "want to peek" always results in my topping the ball rather than getting under it.

"You just keep your head down," my father would say. "I'll watch where your ball lands. It won't be going anywhere if you look up and see."

In other areas of my life I also have a tendency to want to look up and see where things are going. But looking up from the immediate task at hand inevitably brings distraction. I always see so many things to do, which, just for the moment, seem more important than the primary task at hand. Good things.

God tells me, though, to keep my head down. Once I've accomplished that one thing, I can look up and gain direction for the next task. But for now, I need to keep my head down with my eye on the immediate task at hand, trusting him for the future.

Reflect today on any tasks God have given you where you're tempted to peek and get distracted. Imagine, too, you hear your father's voice, calling you to keep committed to that primary task at hand with your eyes clearly focused. He's telling you to keep your head down.

Lessons from the Lake

> *And when he had ceased speaking, he said to Simon, "Put out into the deep and let down your nets for a catch."*

Luke 5:4

When I lived in Canada for several years teaching Parish Nursing, I usually spent time each morning or evening walking along the dirt path at LaSalle Park that borders the bay of Lake Ontario. It was a time to pray, reflect and put the pieces of what I often thought of as a pretty mixed up life into some semblance of order.

The park itself is a delight to the eyes. Waterfowl are plentiful. Canadian geese, ducks of all shapes and sizes and dozens of swans intermingle. They sun themselves on rocks in the heat of the rising sun or float around the bay in the cool of the evening.

One morning I was aware of the ducks darting around, scooping up food from the water's surface. Looking out across the bay I saw at first glance what appeared to be a whole flotilla of little white sailboats. On closer examination I realized, of course, they weren't sailboats at all, but the white tails of all the swans sticking up in the air, just above the surface of the water. The swans' tastes run to deeper things than those of the ducks. The swans dive toward the bottom of the bay with their long graceful necks to search for food and stay there for what seems an eternity.

How often, like the ducks, I'm content to simply skim the surface. I say a quick prayer, read a verse or two from Scripture, rush through my walk. I have a quick quiet time and call it a day, neglecting the good food God has for me lying deeper beneath the surface of his Word and his works of creation. I need to go deeper, drink deeply, slow down and meditate more.

"How great are thy works, O Lord! Thy thoughts are very deep!" (Psalm 92:5). The Psalmist meditated on the deep things and the thoughts of God unknown to the person of dull mind (v. 6). Job's friend Zophar, while not particularly supportive or helpful with his advice to Job concerning his suffering, also recognized, like the Psalmist, that the "things of God" were "deep" (Job 11:7). Job, himself, sought to probe those deep things as he wrestled with the meaning of his suffering.

Jesus begins his call to the disciples by speaking about deep things. "Put out into the deep," he tells Peter. "Let down your nets for a catch." Peter obeys, and the rest is history. *Astonished* is the word used to describe Peter's reaction to the result of his reluctant obedience. Nets broke as Peter and his fellow fishermen cast them into the deep and gathered in the great catch that was waiting for them at the bottom of the sea, in the deep waters where Jesus had directed them to go.

Lord, don't let me be satisfied with skimming the surface of your Word and your works, but encourage me today to go deeper. Sometimes my mind is lulled into dullness by the fast and readily available food of the world. Give me an appetite, instead, for food that truly satisfies.

Going the Extra Mile

> *But a Samaritan, as he journeyed, came to where he was; and when he saw him, he had compassion…*
>
> Luke 10:33

Dorothy is a home-care nurse. In the summer she's up with the birds and out in her garden gathering flowers to take to one of the elderly women she visits "just to cheer her up a bit."

One day when I called Dorothy (on her day off) she'd just returned from a morning at another client's whose house needed a thorough cleaning after years of neglect; Dorothy had arrived with mops and pails and disinfectant and spent the morning scrubbing and sorting. The net result was ten bags full of garbage and an exceedingly grateful landlord.

Sometimes when I call her she says to call her back. A birthday cake might be due to come out of the oven for a neighbor or yet another client. "So many folks out there without families," she'll often say to me. "Gotta give 'em some hope!"

Going the extra mile. Doing things for clients that aren't exactly in our job description is often *the* most important thing we can do for them that day. Going the extra mile is picking flowers for a depressed elderly woman, which bring tears to her eyes and communicates she's cared about. Going the extra mile is clutter control that ensures that an elderly man, who is pretty neglectful of housework and overwhelmed by his caregiving responsibilities for a wife with dementia, won't be evicted. Going the extra mile is a birthday cake and a card for a disabled Vietnam veteran without a family, telling him that someone remembers he really is somebody's special child. Going the extra mile.

Who are these people who go the extra mile? Samaritans, says Jesus. They're defined first of all by their compassion, that attitude of heart, I think, that impels a person not to cross to the other side of the street when they see someone in trouble but to stop by the side of the road, check out their situation and meet the person's immediate needs. When they see gaping wounds, Samaritans disinfect and dress them, binding them up secure. They aren't particularly concerned with "only what the patient has a right to" based on some pre-established governmental guidelines, but if they see an unmet need, they go the extra mile. If 911 isn't available in their part of the country, they don't wring their hands and say "how awful." Some of them might get involved politically and help make changes in the system or organize some volunteers; sometimes they transport people themselves. They might even offer to spend the night with a person in need, going the extra mile. And they're very generous and also good about follow-up care.

Based on the going rate at inns in Jesus' day (one-twelfth of a denarius) and the value of a denarii (one denarius was one day's wage—the Samaritan offered two), you can figure the Samaritan paid out of pocket for twenty-four days of home care, considerably better than Medicare coverage! "I'll be back," he also said to the innkeeper, "just to make sure he is being well taken care of." (Luke 10:29–37). Talk about going the extra mile!

Lord, today in my busyness, help me remember Dorothy and the tale of the Good Samaritan. Grant me strength and joy for my own journey through nursing and show me creative ways to go the extra mile.

I Want to Go Home

I Want to Go Home

> *The eternal God is your dwelling place, and underneath are the everlasting arms.*
>
> Deuteronomy 33:27

"I want to go home."

How may times have you heard one of your hospitalized patients or an elderly resident on a nursing-home unit say, "I want to go home"? I expect it is one of the most oft repeated phrases in the universe among the sick and aged. We all know, too, it's a favorite expression of children, and we even have a disease named for it—homesickness.

Getting away from home for vacations is something we all enjoy, though it is not generally our homes themselves we look forward to leaving but the responsibilities associated with work or home. The familiarity of our own beds and breakfasts, family and friends we've missed, pets who've missed us and shower us with their own brand of affection when we arrive on our doorsteps safe and sound—these we associate with home.

When I think of spiritual needs in nursing, the three that usually come to mind are meaning and purpose, love and forgiveness. A spiritual need for "home" is another. People have a need for a place of refuge, a haven of security. They have a need to feel safe and sound and cared for.

Moses understood the need for home to be a spiritual need that could only be met by God. He does, in fact, call us to consider our very definition of home, not as a place made of wood, stone or brick but as a personal relationship.

In his final blessing for the children of Israel before his death, Moses reminds them of the character of God, their dwelling place, their home. How powerful an image for a people who were to spend forty years wandering homeless in the wilderness, searching for a home, to be reminded that they were never, in fact, a homeless people. God himself is your dwelling place, Moses reminds them. He cradles you in his arms.

Spend some time today meditating on the image of God as your dwelling place, your home. The Psalmist also reminds us that the Lord has been our dwelling place in all generations (Psalm 90:1) and John's message in Revelation is that the dwelling of God is with men (Revelation 21:3). In Jesus, the Son, God the Father has, in fact, come to make his very home in our midst to dwell among us. The future promise associated with that dwelling, for those who believe, is to wipe away all our tears and bring an end to mourning, crying, pain and death (Revelation 21:4).

As you meditate today on the image of God as your dwelling place and on God's everlasting arms underneath you, all around you, supporting you, pray for opportunities to communicate that same reality to those who cross your path daily in hospitals and nursing homes who "want to go home." Pray that as they come to know the depth of their Father's everlasting love for them, they might know they are already there.

When You Pass Through

> *When you pass through the waters I will be with you; and through the rivers, they shall not overwhelm you; when you walk through the fire you shall not be burned, and the flame shall not consume you. For I am the Lord your God, the Holy one of Israel, your Savior.*
>
> Isaiah 43:2–3a

Waters of our lives. Rivers. Fire. Flame. We all have those moments in our nursing careers and in our personal lives when we're certain we're not going to make it. Not if we have to go *through*. But God says through is the route to take.

I would prefer an alternate route, avoiding those moments altogether. I do not want to go through trouble. I don't want to confront that unjust situation at work that may cost me my job if I share my views. I don't want to admit my guilt and be totally honest with my spouse. I don't want to tell my kids no.

But God is telling me in Isaiah to remember what happened in the Red Sea and the fiery furnace. So I close my eyes today and visualize history. I am one of the Israelites standing by the Red Sea. The enemy's pursuing. I look at the waves, and I want to go back to Egypt. God knows my fears and gives a strong command to Moses. "Tell the people of Israel to go forward" (Exodus 14:15), so off I finally go, with the rest of my cowardly comrades. Fearfully, hesitantly, but *through*. I can picture the waves, rising up around me on each side. There's no time to build an ark and no alternate route available. I can't look back. The enemy pursues. But I am passing *through*. And God is with me, behind, before me. I reach the other side.

My thoughts are now with Daniel's three friends in the fiery furnace. Bowing down to idols was not an option for them, and they know they have to go *through*. They are thrown, bound, into a furnace, and flames surround them as they fall.

But as I gaze into the fiery furnace, a new image forms. I see the three friends loosed, unbound and walking through the fire, and they are not alone. A fourth person is walking through the fire with them, and they survive (Daniel 3:20–26).

God doesn't say he'll meet me on the other side of the waters and the fire. He says he'll be with me in them, walk with me through them. There's no guarantee of that if I refuse to go or I take an alternate route.

Whatever your problem is today or tomorrow, remember history. Remember the Red Sea. Remember the fiery furnace. Don't be afraid of drowning. Don't be afraid of the flame. God will be with you. Pass through.

Dwelling Among Us

> *And the Word became flesh and dwelt among us, full of grace and truth.*
>
> John 1:14

A number of years ago I wrote a book for caregivers and shared the following story of a nurse who worked in pediatrics.*

One small child on the unit was having difficulty breathing and was confined to an oxygen tent. The child was terrified by the whole experience and made his terror known by crying loudly for his mother. This nurse had a solution to the problem. She lifted up the tent flaps and crawled in beside the screaming toddler. Calmed by her presence, the little boy promptly fell asleep.

When I was reminded of that story I was a caregiver for my mother, who had Alzheimer's disease, and also, during the same time period, for my father, who had cancer. I often felt a lot like that little boy in the oxygen tent. Other caregivers can describe similar feelings. At times we've desperately longed for someone to "climb into our tents" with us to give us comfort, encouragement and the reassurance that everything will be OK. Long-term caregiving for loved ones can seem like a suffocating experience. You want to escape and get away from the four confining walls of home. You want to be free of all the responsibilities and fears.

As I look back on that experience of caregiving, I realize there were many people who came into my life and crawled into my tent with me.

Sometimes relatives came and shared funny stories about the past when we were all together as an extended family. Though my mother no longer was able to remember, these were times of laughter, reminiscence and healing for my father and me.

Sometimes home health aides came. They quite literally dwelt in our home for hours at a time so I could go out and shop, continue to work, or even relax and play a round of golf.

Sometimes members from our church came and brought with them prayers and baskets of food to sustain us spiritually and physically. These friends would also remind me that there was also an ultimate resource who was already dwelling with us.

About two thousand years ago Jesus opened the tent flaps and came into a world that was having difficulty breathing, a world that sat in darkness and the shadow of death. He spent his time with the sick, the suffering, with people in need of healing. He also spent time with their caregivers. He wept with Mary and Martha (John 11:33–35). He entered Simon's house and healed Simon's mother-in-law (Luke 4:38–39). He responded to the need of Jairus, the father of the twelve-year-old girl who was dying, going with him to his home (Mark 5:22–24).

Lord, help me remember the next time I'm feeling overwhelmed and confined as a caregiving daughter or son, mother or father, husband or wife, or nurse with a patient in need, that you are my ultimate resource. Thank you for sharing our tents of affliction, calming us with your presence, dwelling among us.

*Adapted from Sharon Fish. *Alzheimer's: Caring for Your Loved One, Caring for Yourself.* (Harold Shaw Publishers, 1996).

He Will Carry You

> *...even to your old age I am He, and to gray hairs I will carry you. I have made, and I will bear; I will carry and will save.*

Isaiah 46:4

He spoke to me of his longing to "always go to the Holy Land" and how this had finally become a reality. At the time of the trip he was "suffering from a crippling arthritis" but was accompanied by "some of my young friends who helped me and sometimes carried me." He spoke repeatedly of his gratefulness to God for allowing him to go to Israel and of his thankfulness for his "brothers in Christ" for "taking care of me."

My interview for a course I was taking in nursing research was winding down. Mr. Laton [introduced in "The Promise Box"], age eighty-nine, was an immigrant from Latvia. He spoke to me in halting English. Throughout the interview he had painted pictures for me of his life, first in Latvia as a young boy and then in America as a young man. Now he was telling me of his recent experience in Israel, the land of his longing.

As I reflect back on that interview, I can easily picture Mr. Laton sitting at his kitchen table. Hunched over, he still suffered from arthritis, a condition he viewed as a "small, insignificant problem." I can also imagine him in Israel, surrounded by the students he loved from the church around the corner where he now lived. I can see, in my mind's eye, two of the strongest students making a "chair" with their crossed-over arms, lifting him up and transporting him through the Old City, perhaps down the Way of the Cross. I can picture them winding down the rocky path to the Dead Sea or up to the garden tomb, gently but firmly lifting him up and carrying him where he wanted to go.

The prophet Isaiah paints a beautiful and tender picture of people being carried in the arms of the Lord. It's a good image for nurses to meditate on. While a good goal in nursing is to help the people we care for regain their independence, the reality is that many will always need total or partial assistance and be dependent on us or on others to meet their daily needs. God would remind both them and us that he is the One we are all ultimately dependent on.

"...in his love and in his pity he redeemed them; he lifted them up and carried them all the days of old," wrote Isaiah (Isaiah 63:9). Love and pity are attitudes from the heart of our Father. Compassion, a unique combination of both, was the primary motivating factor that moved God to care for the people he created. Compassion to bear, to carry, to lift up and save.

Lord, help me today to communicate your compassion to those in my care, especially the elderly, the frail and those with crippling diseases. And when my own hair is gray, help me remember that you are the one who bears me up and will one day lift me up in your arms, carrying me into your presence.

Enabling a Meeting

He leads me beside still waters; he restores my soul.

Psalm 23:2

Stephen Ames asked me to stay for a few minutes. He wanted to talk, about his cancer and about his fears. So I stayed and listened. I also asked him if he would like me to pray for him. He said yes. He hadn't been to church "in years and years and years," but he did want me to pray.

I remember feeling overwhelmed by this man's need. I reached over the side of the bed and placed my hand on his shoulder and began to pray the Twenty-third Psalm, turning each phrase into a personal prayer request.

"Lord, show Stephen you are his shepherd. Lead him beside your still waters. Restore his soul."

Suddenly I was realized I was not the only one in the room praying. Stephen was too. At first he began to silently weep. Then he began to sob—huge, wracking sobs that shook the bed. Then he cried out loud for God to forgive him, a cry to restore his soul. The next day I brought him a large-print Bible, read him some other Psalms and left it by his bedside table. Two weeks later Stephen died.

Spirituality is no longer a neglected need in nursing. Many nurses are turning to practices like yoga, Therapeutic Touch, and to various forms of Eastern meditation and equating these practices with spiritual care. The focus is on quieting the mind and turning attention inward, to what is believed to be our own inherent divinity or own spiritual center to facilitate our own spiritual healing or the healing of others.

Dietrich Bonhoeffer, author of a book for pastors on spiritual care,* had a decidedly different view, believing that the main end of the spiritual-care process is to enable a meeting between Christ and the person to take place.

Bonhoeffer believed that the only purpose of spiritual care is to enable this life-giving meeting to occur; then one should step aside gracefully and allow the conversation to go on—the conversation between the person in need and God. God alone meets the deepest needs of the heart and is the true restorer of the soul. Not the pastor, not the nurse, but God.

Lord, today as I care for the people you created and love, teach me the true meaning of spiritual care. Give me opportunities to pray for those I care for, then to step gracefully aside and enable the conversation to go on—their conversation with you.

*Dietrich Bonhoeffer. *Spiritual Care.* Trans. by Jay C. Rochelle. (Fortress Press, 1985), p. 11.

The Apple of His Eye

> *He found him in a desert land, and in the howling waste of the wilderness; he encircled him, he cared for him, he kept him as the apple of his eye.*
>
> Deuteronomy 32:10

Books on the topic of caring are legion in nursing, stressing the need to recapture this art in the midst of a highly technological society where people are often viewed as an amalgamation of body parts to be separately serviced by any number of specialists. We are reminded that we not only must care but are given countless tips on how to do it, as if caring was a concept foreign to nurses.

Caring, however, though perhaps in need of some redefining, has never been a foreign concept in nursing, and it is certainly not a foreign concept to God. One of the most beautiful illustrations is found in Deuteronomy 32:10, a song of God's care for his people in the wilderness—people like Allen Blaine.

Depression hit Allen Blaine hard when his wife died and he relocated to a nursing home. He felt unloved and uncared for by God and readily expressed those feelings to the nursing staff both in words and in behavior, frequently lying in bed, sobbing. He regularly attended church services in the home but needed more constant reminders, during the week, of God's continued faithfulness and care for him, and of God's promise to bring him out of the howling waste of the wilderness experience he perceived the nursing home to be.

Reminiscence helped him to eventually recapture a glimpse of God's love, as he was encouraged to share stories with the staff and with other residents of God's provision for himself and his wife during the forty years they had spent in Africa as missionaries. Many of those days, too, had been wilderness experiences, yet Allen and his wife, Mildred, both knew that God had called them to that place and was watching over them. Hovering over them like a mother eagle, God had encircled them with his love and care and kept them safe as apples of his eye, his own, his cherished possessions.

Verses 11–12 of Deuteronomy 32 extend this image of a caring God. "Like an eagle that stirs up its nest, that flutters over its young, spreading out its wings, catching them, bearing them on its pinions, the Lord alone did lead …" This image of God adds a new dimension of caring, that of the mother eagle training her young ones for flight. As Allen reflected on the countless times they had experienced protection as God tipped them out of the nest and let them try their wings, but also kept them from plummeting to the ground, he was gently reminded that this new nursing home experience was also a training flight and that Allen Blaine was still God's child. As in days gone by, God was still there to bear him up and break the fall. Allen Blaine was still his cherished possession.

Lord, help me communicate your character and your care for those entrusted to my care in nursing as they walk through wilderness experiences. Let me point them to you as the One who encircles them with your love, and will bear them up when they fall.

It's Not the Dying Part

> *And when I go and prepare a place for you, I will come again and will take you to myself, that where I am you may be also.*

John 14:3

Sarah Williams was seventy-five and in the end stages of amyotrophic lateral sclerosis, more commonly known as ALS or Lou Gehrig's disease. I had been called in to consult. The staff had given up, judging from the notes on the charts. "Always complaining." "Never satisfied." "You can never do enough for her." "Demanding." Nursing assistants frequently requested to care for people other than Sarah, and some refused to care for her altogether. The ones that did care for her would respond to her call-bell, carefully reposition her and then leave the room. Within five minutes her call-bell would be on again. "I'm still not comfortable," Sarah would say. "Please help me turn over."

"They oughta put a revolving door in her room," one of the aides said to me. I cared for Sarah too, relieving the aides. After spending several evenings with her, responding to her call-bell, repositioning her time after time, just as the staff had described, I asked her how she really felt and she told me she was dying. "But it's not the dying part, but the dying alone that bothers me," she said.

Dying alone. Sarah's need really wasn't for repositioning but for people. She constantly demanded attention because she didn't want to be alone in her room, didn't want to die alone. One practical solution presented itself—a special recliner so Sarah could spend time out of the room, sitting next to the nurses' station, and a move from a private to a semi-private room. Sarah got to be near people, and her demands for constant repositioning ceased. The recliner also enabled her to come to the weekly Bible studies and church services in the home, something she had not done before. Sarah also got to be near Jesus.

"Don't be troubled in heart," Jesus told his disciples. "I'm going to prepare a place especially for you, a home with many rooms. It's my Dad's home, actually, and we want you to come and live with us. But I can also offer you something else—a traveling companion for the journey; you won't need to make the journey to see us alone. When you're ready, I'll come again and take you with me to be with my Father. I am the way to get there. I'll be with you on the road home."

"Even though I walk through the valley of the shadow of death, I fear no evil; for thou art with me" (Psalm 23:4). David knew the way that Jesus spoke of and was comforted by the promise of a traveling companion for the journey. I suspect the disciples did too, after awhile, once Jesus' words finally sank into their hearts. And so, at the end of her life, did Sarah.

Father, today in my nursing, help me be aware of people who may not know they can have a traveling companion for the journey through the shadow of death, who may be afraid of dying alone, unsure of their destination and the specific route. Help me to show them the way.

Rooming In

And the Word became flesh and dwelt among us, full of grace and truth…

John 1:14

Making sense of the gospel and explaining it to others requires a search for metaphors. The writers of the Bible used them freely, realizing no single metaphor could express a full understanding of God's redemptive activity. Taken together, however, metaphors could provide us with a more complete understanding of the Christian life and gospel story. Nursing, too, is rich in metaphors that can help us tell the story, like the metaphor of rooming in.

Rooming in. Nurses in obstetrics are familiar with the concept as significant others join the expectant mother to support her through the labor experience. Many pediatric units also encourage parents to spend not only days but nights in their children's rooms, rendering care, calming their fears.

As a graduate student I worked as a research assistant on a project that incorporated the concept of rooming in for adult surgical patients. Families and loved ones were enrolled in a study to determine if staying overnight in the room of an older person following orthopedic surgery would make a difference with respect to variables like confusion, pain and amount and type of medication needed.

John also begins his gospel with the metaphor of rooming in, of the Word becoming flesh and dwelling among us. Jesus came into our hurting world to be with us, to live with us, to stay with us, to care for us. Not only did Jesus come to dwell with us but he came to dwell in us, to room in with us. "And the Word became flesh and dwelt among us," John tells us.

Paul, too, writes of this rooming in experience, of Christ dwelling in our hearts through faith (Ephesians 3:17).

This rooming in experience will also be the experience of the believer in the future: God with us, dwelling among us, tenderly caring for us. In the midst of the labor, in the midst of the pain and distress associated with sickness and death, the dwelling of God is with those who suffer and hurt. "He will dwell with them, and they shall be his people, and God himself with be with them; he will wipe away every tear from their eyes, and death shall be no more, neither shall there be mourning nor crying nor pain any more, for the former things have passed away" (Revelation 21:3–4).

Rooming in. Spend some time this week reflecting on this and other metaphors in nursing that can help you understand God's redemptive activity, and pray for opportunities to share with others.

After Hours

> *And Simon answered, "Master: we toiled all night and took nothing! But at your word I will let down the nets."*
>
> Luke 5:5

Eight-hour shifts are rare in nursing; in the hospital there's always the call bell that buzzes the exact minute you're ready to walk out the door. Then there's the paperwork to chart. In the nursing home there's the resident who calls to you just as you're getting on the elevator. "Nurse! Oh, nurse!" In home care it's your supervisor calling you on your day off about a newly discharged patient the agency decided to cover and they're short one nurse. "Would you please work this morning, just for a couple hours?"

After hours. It's easy for me to grumble and complain. I'd rather just get on the elevator, close the door, smile and wave. Sometimes I do. I'd rather not answer the phone on my day off. Sometimes I don't. But sometimes I begin to think about all the things that have happened—after hours.

It was after hours, after they had fished all night and caught nothing, that the disciples cast out their nets just one more time and caught enough to sink their boat.

It was after hours, after twelve long years and many hours of misery and worthless remedies, that a woman with an issue of blood came up and touched the hem of Jesus' robe and was healed.

It was after hours, after years and years of tears, that Hannah conceived and bore the fervently prayed for Samuel, and that Sarah conceived and bore Isaac, her child of spring-time, her child of promise.

It was after hours, after waiting and praying in an upper room in Jerusalem, that the followers of Jesus received the power of the Holy Spirit to bear witness to their resurrected Lord.

I remember, too, that it was sometimes after hours that I've had time to pray with a newly admitted nursing-home resident who was troubled to be there, anxious about her future, grieving over the loss of her home. I remember, too, that it was sometimes after hours I had more time to spend with the home-care client who was living alone, fearful about having another heart attack and in need of someone to sit and listen without worrying about the need to run off to the next client.

"Nurse! Oh, nurse!" The next time, Lord, I hear someone calling me as I'm about to step in the elevator, or hear the telephone ring early on a Sunday morning, let me not begrudge the time it takes to spend with those who need my time—after hours.

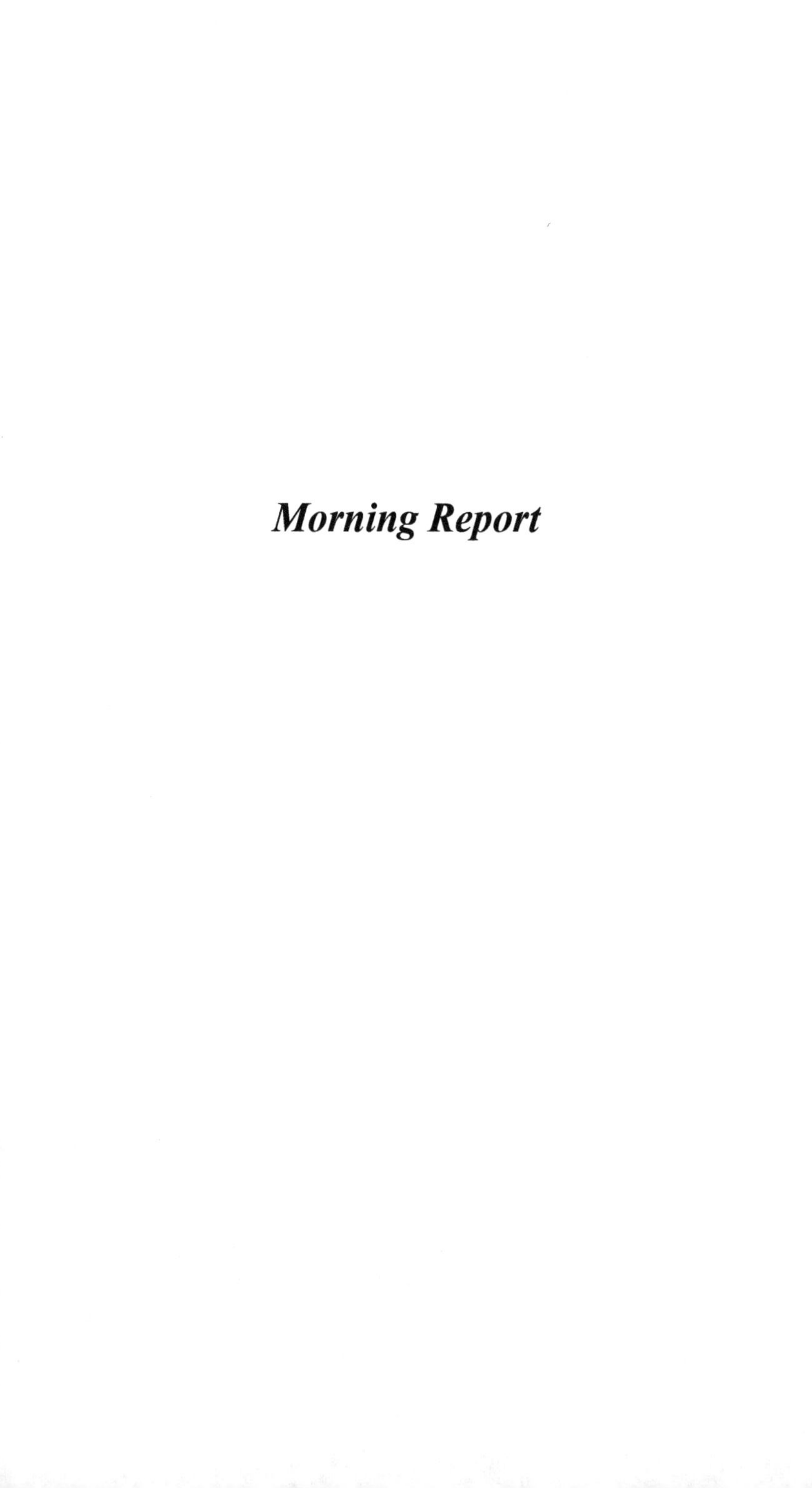

Morning Report

Morning Report

> *The Lord God has given me the tongue of those who are taught, that I may know how to sustain with a word him that is weary. Morning by morning he wakens, he wakens my ear to hear as those who are taught.*
>
> Isaiah 50:4

It's seven o'clock in the morning and time for daily report. We find out what IV's have infiltrated, which patients are scheduled for surgery and who spent the night in pain.

The time for report may vary, depending on our shift, but the focus is the same—the needs of those in our care and what our responsibilities are for them. Few of us would imagine beginning our shift without this ritual of reporting. It's as routine a practice as brushing our teeth.

Morning report is not always a quiet time. In the hospital or nursing-home setting it's impossible to escape the call bells of needy people demanding attention, or the bells and whistles on monitors and respirators if we work in an ICU or emergency room. Yet even with the interruptions, we know there's one thing we must do before beginning our daily routine: listen to report.

God also reminds us of the importance of morning report and even puts this reminder in the appropriate context of caregiving. "Morning by morning he wakens, he wakens my ear to hear as those who are taught," wrote the prophet Isaiah (Isaiah 50:4). One result of that time alone with God, in the quiet hours of the morning, evening, or, for some of us, the middle of the night, is an increased ability to comfort others and "to sustain with a word him that is weary." What a wonderful promise to know that as we simply spend some quiet moments with God with our own ears open to be taught by him through his Word, he will enable us to speak words of comfort and encouragement to others. We can nourish others with the same Word we feed on. We can comfort others with the same Word our own spirits are strengthened by. We can more easily bear the burdens of others as we find our own burdens lifted in our times alone with God.

Distractions to dissuade us from these quiet times with God are many. At home we are all plagued by our own versions of bells and whistles. Again Isaiah helps us consider the importance of this time away, of setting our "face like a flint" (v. 7) focused on the Lord alone, his will and his Word. "The Lord God has opened my ear," he writes, "and I was not rebellious, I turned not backward" (v. 5). For me, it always takes a bit of effort to make that time and come apart. I need the reminder that not only will I benefit personally from this discipline, but it can carry over to the people I care for.

Pray today that your ears would be wakened to hear and be taught by the Lord. Pray, too, for God to direct you specifically to those who might need your care at work in the form of a prayer, extra time to listen to needs and fears or perhaps a word of encouragement from your own "morning report" with God.

One Happy Thing

> *Look at the birds of the air: they neither sow nor reap nor gather into barns, and yet your heavenly Father feeds them. Are you not of more value than they?*
>
> Matthew 6:26

"Martha, can you think of at least one happy thing today?"

"No," she wailed. "I'm so upset!"

"Not one?"

"I said, no!"

My plans to cheer up Martha Stevens were not going well. Most afternoons when I came to work Martha would be sitting in her rocking chair. Often she'd be crying, and today was no exception. Sometimes I could lift her mood a bit with the offer of something to eat. Usually, though, Martha sat and sobbed. Then one day the social worker brought in a parakeet and hung the cage next to the window in Martha's room. Suddenly Martha stopped crying. She started smiling. A tiny parakeet had become Martha's "happy thing."

I can identify with Martha. It's easy, at times, to just sit and sob, and hard to think of happy things.

Assessing the specific cause of Martha's anxiety was difficult, due to her cognitive impairment. Assessing my own root cause of anxiety is far easier. It's often the state of being overwhelmed, of having said "yes" to one too many demands, then suffering the consequences of those decisions. Fears about the future can also trigger anxiety.

Jesus understands those fears. Men and women he came to reveal the Father to were also anxious and troubled. Reasons for anxiety seemed concrete, related to personal economic woes. Would there be food? Would there be clothing? Would there be money for bills? These are present day realities in nursing, too, with budget cuts threatening our jobs and even the very existence of the institutions we work for.

What are your anxieties today? What are those things that move you to weep and wail like Martha? Make a list of them and then go for a walk.

Listen, as you walk, to the birds. Also look at them, as Jesus recommended. They, too, have to feed themselves and provide for their young. But they do it, it seems, with ease. Instinctively they know that what they need is available to them, provided by their heavenly Father. They know God will feed them as they go about the business of the day.

Look, too, as you walk, at the flowers. "Consider the lilies of the field, how they grow," recommends Jesus (Matthew 6:28). Arrayed, they are greater than Solomon in all his glory. Instinctively they turn their petals to the sun, trumpeting their praise to their heavenly Father, who clothes and cares for them.

Jesus calls us to focus our attention not on our anxieties but on the smallest, simplest, most insignificant things in his creation and on the Father's lavish provisions and loving concern for them. He tells us to not be worried at all and to refrain from looking inward.

The next time I find myself weeping and wailing and hanging onto the Kleenex box, trying to think of at least one happy thing, I hope I remember Martha and her parakeet and my need to go for a walk.

Field Notes

> *For whatever was written in former days was written for our instruction, that by steadfastness and by the encouragement of the scriptures we might have hope.*

Romans 15:4

Nursing students in graduate school are required to take a number of elective courses to round out their studies. For my own doctoral program I wound up taking courses in anthropology. We studied people and we studied culture. The anthropological concept that intrigued me the most was that of the "field note."

Field notes, simply defined, are any notes an anthropologist makes about the people and the culture when he or she is "in the field." Usually they consist of quick scribblings on pieces of paper or three-by-five cards that can be filed for later retrieval. In more leisurely times the researcher rereads and reconstructs the notes, fills in the gaps and writes a book or an article. The field notes themselves act as memory joggers; without them, much of what was observed in the field and the serendipitous insights gained that would later be important for a more accurate analysis would simply be forgotten or dimly remembered.

Field notes are also important to keep in our Christian walk. I think of these as spiritual memory joggers, the everyday occurrences of our own lives and culture, specifically as they pertain to our relationship with God. Documenting any aspect of our daily lives may seem like the last thing we want to do, given the stack of paperwork we're already faced with at work. We need, then, to keep it simple. In a daily or weekly log or diary, jot down brief reflections about whatever it is God may have done in your life. What special insight did you gain from

Scripture? What prayers were prayed and answered? What struggles are you having in your spiritual life? How did God help you with those struggles?

Spiritual field notes are important documents for the Christian. When times get tough for us in the future, as they inevitably will, our scribbled notes about God's involvement in our lives are memory joggers. We can trust him in the present and future as we reflect on his past faithfulness to us in the concrete "raw data" of our lives versus only dimly remembered ways.

The Scriptures themselves are a type of field note, documentation or running log of the lives and times of our ancestors, some of whom took time out to document their own walk with God or to relate stories of their observations. In Romans Paul writes that by steadfastness and the encouragement of these field notes we may have hope, because they point us to the God of steadfastness and encouragement.

Lord, help me today to take a few minutes to document what you've been doing for me and teaching me from your Word as a future encouragement when I need to be reminded to be steadfast. Keep me writing those field notes!

Sairey Gamp and Betsy Prig

> *But thanks be to God, who in Christ always leads us in triumph, and through us spreads the fragrance of the knowledge of him everywhere.*

2 Corinthians 2:14

If you've ever taken an undergraduate nursing history course, you're probably familiar with two of our infamous fictional ancestors—Sairey Gamp, the night nurse, and Betsy Prig, the day nurse. They were both looking for an easy way to make a living and graced the pages of Dickens' novel, *Martin Chuzzlewit.** They preferred to do their caregiving, such as it was, in the homes of people who shared the same disease and were reasonably well-off. "The pickled salmon...is quite delicious. I can partick'ler recommend it" and "The easy-chair ain't soft enough. You'll want this piller" was Betsy's idea of change of shift report to a usually inebriated Sairey. Dickens describes Sairey as bearing a "peculiar fragrance" that smelled like wine vaults. Neither would have been hired today as community health nurses, had references been checked.

Nursing, like any other profession, is not without its share of Sairey Gamps and Betsy Prigs, who bear peculiar fragrances and seem to practice the profession of sloth.

Paul teaches us a different way. All Christians are to bear peculiar fragrances and we often do so, not in pleasant and easy circumstances where the food is rich and the furniture is comfortable, but in the midst of hardship and difficulty.

Paul's introductory remarks to the church at Corinth describe the affliction of the disciples in graphic terms: "...we were so utterly, unbearably crushed that we despaired of life itself," he writes (2 Corinthians: 1:8). They even felt they had received the "sentence of death" (v. 9). But their perceived death sentence and very real difficulties had a purpose. They were to cause them to rely on God and not on themselves, on the God who even had the power to resurrect. They could trust the God who had delivered them in the past to deliver them again in the present. He was a God who always led in triumph.

The fragrance night-nurse Sairey spread, wrote Dickens, was "borne upon the breeze," as if a "passing fairy," who had previously been to the wine-vaults, "had hiccoughed." The fragrance the Christian is to bear is also to be borne upon the breeze. The image Paul gives us in Corinthians, however, is not one of stale, sweet-smelling wine from a passing fairy but that of a pungent and sweet-smelling burning of incense that gives off a pleasing odor, rising up and drawing other people to the knowledge of Christ as they see God in Christ, working out his purposes in our difficult lives and bringing us through victoriously.

Lord, today let me be a sweet-smelling aroma to those I work with and those I care for. Help me, too, to trust you, working out your good and perfect will in the midst of difficulties at home and work, showing me your resurrection power and leading me in triumph.

*Charles Dickens. *Martin Chuzzlewit.* Chapter 25. (*The Penguin Classics,* 1843/2000).

Diseases of the Heart

> *He does not deal with us according to our sins, nor requite us according to our iniquities.*
>
> Psalm 103:10

Twentieth-century literature also has its share of infamous nurses. One of the most famous is Nurse Ratched, otherwise known as the "Big Nurse," in charge of a ward in a mental hospital in Ken Kesey's novel, *One Flew Over the Cuckoo's Nest.** Sairey Gamp and Betsy Prig wouldn't have lasted long under Nurse Ratched's supervision. She was a veritable tyrant who ran her ward like a "precision-made machine." Nurse Ratched was domineering and manipulative. She exploited people's fears, frightening them into submission with exposure of their secret sins and human weaknesses. She demanded perfection and she got it.

Secret sins and human weaknesses: in addition to suffering from more visible diseases like diabetes, cancer and strokes, some of the people we care for may suffer from diseases of the heart. As nurses we have them too, those areas of our lives we want no one else to know about, our areas of secret shame and vulnerability. None of us would fare very well on Nurse Ratched's ward.

Thankfully we have a God who deals with us much differently than Nurse Ratched. He, too, wants to expose our sins and weakness, but not exploitatively for all the world to see. The Lord, instead, would bring us to a place of healing with conviction, not frightening us into submission by condemnation.

King David was well acquainted with secret sins. In 2 Samuel 11 we read of his abuse of power and position and of his conniving and scheming to cover up an adulterous affair and avoid a public scandal. Soon David would know the severe judgment of God upon his secret sin, but also God's forgiveness as he repented, and God's grace that strengthened him for future service.

One of the problems of secret sin is the clingyness of it; shame always seems to hang around, reminding us, as Nurse Ratched did her patients, of our frailty and failure. But when we come to the Lord and confess our sin, our transgressions are removed, as far as the east is from the west (Psalm 103:12). There's no more need for shame. The God David praises in Psalm 103 is a God of compassion who healed his disease of the heart and crowned him with steadfast love and mercy.

For a more extended quiet time today or sometime this week, spend more time with David. Read Psalm 103 in its entirety, and turn it into your own personal prayer. Hear the Lord saying to you, "I'll forgive all your iniquity and heal the diseases of your heart, even your secret sins and human weaknesses."

*Ken Kesey. *One Flew Over the Cuckoo's Nest.* (Viking Press, 1962).

Turn Right at the Chicken Coop

How great are his signs, how mighty his wonders!

Daniel 4:3

How do I get to your house?" I asked.

"Turn right at the chicken coop. Then drive about five miles until you come to an old rusty tractor out in the field. Turn left. Ten minutes down that road you'll come to a fork. Bear right and follow the road to the pond. After the pond you'll see the house. You can't miss it. It's the only one on the road."

Working in community health in rural upstate New York, I frequently needed directions. They were usually quite descriptive. People would orient me to where they lived by describing visible signposts. A chicken coop. A pond. An old, rusty tractor.

God is also a God of visible signposts. Throughout history he seemed to delight in giving his people signs. One of the first was a bow in the cloud that reminded his people of his covenant with them for all generations to come. The Sabbath was a sign that spoke of the need for rest and refreshment. Twelve stones were a sign for the Israelites, when they crossed over the Jordan River, that their God was awesome and mighty.

Over and over signs appear in the sky. There were stars too numerous to number that God displayed to Abraham as a sign of a promised son; a sun stood still for Joshua to assure him of victory in battle; a star in the East guided wise men to their Savior.

In the Gospels we read about the flip side to signs. People demanded visible signs in order to believe. Jesus discouraged people from believing in him simply because of the miracles he accomplished, yet nevertheless, signs and wonders were done by Jesus and, later, by the apostles, communicating a clear message that God was in their midst.

Nurses working in rural community health need clear and certain signs. Working in the inner city, signs are helpful too. Knowing that Sam Smith lives on 42nd and Vine is useful information, but knowing he also lives next to the doughnut shop and across from the auto-parts store is even more helpful. Being a nurse with a poor sense of direction, I always appreciate those specific signs.

Though there's little encouragement in Scripture to specifically seek signs in order to prove God's power or existence, there is much encouragement to pay attention to the signs God himself gives us daily that reveal more of his ways and will for us.

What signs do you need from God today: clear and certain guidance from his Word or greater awareness of the circumstances orchestrated by God to point you in a needed direction for your life? As you reflect on God's signs, may the assurance you receive as you commit your way to the Lord, asking for his direction, be as clear as the assurance of some of my home-care clients. You can't miss it, they often tell me. It's the only one on the road.

Dew Drops and Gentle Rain

> *May my teaching drop as the rain, my speech distill as the dew, as the gentle rain upon the tender grass, and as the showers upon the herb.*
>
> Deuteronomy 32:2

Nurses have many roles and they often overlap. One primary role is teaching. We may teach students in classrooms and clinical situations. We teach principles and practices of health promotion and prevention to patients in hospitals and clients in homes. We teach family members how to draw up insulin or change dressings. And we really want them to pay attention to what we say.

Books and articles abound today in nursing on how to teach, but for the money, the book of Deuteronomy remains one of the best. The author's credentials are impressive, too. Moses was no novice, but a 120-year-old expert and still a teacher at heart, responsible to pass his wisdom on.

"May my teaching drop as the rain," said Moses. He spoke words that penetrated and sank in deep. That's what we want when we teach students. We want them to remember the concepts and principles, to ponder them in their minds, hide them in their hearts and apply them.

"May my speech distill as the dew." Like Moses with his charges, the Israelites, we want our patients and their families to retain only the part that is essential in the teaching; we try and keep our directions as clear and uncomplicated as possible. As dew is refreshing as it waters the early morning earth, we'd like to think our teaching made a difference in and improved the lives of those we teach and care for.

Moses likened his teaching to gentle rain falling on tender grass and to showers upon the herb. He had an understanding of his hearers and was sensitive to their needs. Students we teach may appear strong and self-confident on the outside, but inside they are often a bundle of insecurities. If we remember our own years as nursing students, new grads or new faculty, we were insecure, too.

Students of any age need to be taught with gentleness. So we try to teach with a gentle authority, seeking to bring out the best in our students, stretching their minds and bending them but not breaking them, watering them so they'll bloom and become teachers themselves of patients, families and perhaps other students. Patients and families are often in crisis, too, and "bundles of nerves." They're fearful of the time when they have to give their first injection or change their first dressing alone, without the patient presence and verbal directions of their nurse. They need firm and clear and gentle teaching. They need to be told it will be OK.

Moses wasn't teaching nursing but he was teaching about spiritual health. All the assembly of Israel heard his teaching. He focused on one theme only and kept it simple. Moses' theme was God. Proclaiming the name of the Lord was his only objective; ascribing greatness to the Lord was his only goal. Clear and simple directions.

Physical Therapy

And Jesus in pity touched...

Matthew 20:34a

Reach out and touch someone" is a phrase everyone who has a television set is well acquainted with, thanks to the advertising of one phone company. Touching by phone is a very good thing to do. But physical touch is also important. It's a means of communicating caring.

I'm writing this an hour after returning from a worship service in a nearby nursing home where I volunteer. After the service the nursing home chaplain made the rounds of the wheelchair-bound residents, shaking hands and hugging. Many of the residents, both men and women, would reach out to him as well with a warm embrace, thanking him with tears in their eyes for coming. In the middle of his sermon a woman with dementia became agitated; I went over, put an arm around her, then stroked her hand. She quieted immediately and remained quiet and seemed content through the rest of the service. Touch, physical touch.

Reach out and touch. Jesus did it often. He touched people for healing. He stretched out his hand and touched the lepers, and they were cleansed. He touched people lying sick with fever, and they were restored to health. He touched the eyes of blind, and they were opened. He touched the dead, and they were raised. He didn't always heal by touching, it wasn't a magic formula, but often he did, reaching out to the loneliness of the leper, to the aches and pain of the woman tossing and turning with fever, to the isolation of the blind, to the grief of families mourning their loved ones. The touch of Jesus was wholistic. It restored people to physical health but also to relationships with others and to their environment.

Reach out and touch. God always has. He touches people for service. He "put forth his hand" and touched the mouth of Jeremiah (Jeremiah 1:9). He touched Daniel and sent him trembling to his knees, calling him "greatly beloved," assuring him of answered prayer (Daniel 10:10–12).

Reach out and touch. God always will. He touches people for comfort. He reaches out to touch his people, reaches out to "hold [their] right hand," tells them to "fear not," says, "I will help you" (Isaiah 41:13).

In today's world of nursing where the paradigm has shifted, for many, to a focus on a variety of occult practices including rebalancing energy fields with non-contact forms of touch and nurses' hands that wave and hover over the body, it's good to remember in contrast the biblical heritage of physical touch and the importance of the physical human body that God himself created. God formed us, knit us together, touching us even in our mother's womb (Psalm 139). He continues to fashion us like clay. He molds us, remakes us, reshapes us. The imagery is physical.

Lord, today I would hold up my hands and offer them to you. Help me to use them wisely and well, communicating your tender care and power to heal and to save to the lonely, the sick, the isolated, the dying. Touch me today, for your service.

The Royal Touch

And he stretched out his hand and touched him, saying, "I will; be clean." And immediately his leprosy was cleansed.

Matthew 8:3

During the Middle Ages, in England and France, royal succession was considered a divine right. One accompaniment of that right was believed to be the ability of the monarch to heal through prayers and by physical touch, commonly known as "handing." The malady most commonly believed to be cured by a touch from a king or queen was scrofula, a disfiguring type of tuberculosis that affected the lymph glands of the neck and manifested as a skin disease accompanied by swollen glands, suppuration and occasional scarring. There are numerous historical references to various monarchs engaging in this practice; it was called the practice of the King's Touch for the King's Evil and sometimes the Royal Touch.

One account was written in 1575, by a man who witnessed Queen Elizabeth exercising this healing rite. "By her Highnes' accustomed mercy and charittee 9 were cured of the peynfull and dangerous deseaz called the King's Evil; for that Kings and Queens of the Realm without other medicin save only by handing and prayers only doe cure it," wrote this historian of the times. Charles II was said to have touched 92,107 people for healing from May 1660 to May 1680. "When I consider his Majestie's gracious touch" and "his marvellous miraculous method of healing," the King's surgeon wrote, "more souls have been healed by his Majestie's sacred touch in one year than have ever been cured by all the physicians of his three kingdoms ever since his happy restoration."*

Scrofula today is not a disease we're acquainted with in nursing, but we are acquainted with others that manifest with similar symptoms, diseases that disfigure, that isolate, that cause people *without* the disease to shun those *with* the disease out of fear or out of ignorance.

The kings and sometimes the queens, though, touched people with scrofula and appeared to touch quite often. Paintings of that era depict royalty receiving the sacrament of communion prior to going out into the courtyard to touch for healing people that society had deemed untouchable.

Nurses who are Christians can identify; we, too, know something of "divine right" as members of a royal and holy priesthood of believers. "Handing" is also part of our heritage both as Christians and as nurses, reaching out to touch the untouchable. It's basic Christianity and Nursing 101.

Today in your nursing and in your community, take time to be aware of those considered untouchable by the world and pray that they might experience the Royal Touch of Jesus in their lives, through you, perhaps, or through other Christians reaching out to comfort and to heal.

*From an address delivered before the Erie [Pennsylvania] County Medical Society by W. Flint, January 7, 1851. Printed at the office of the *Chronicle*.

In Our Weakness

In Our Weakness

> *Likewise the Spirit helps us in our weakness; for we do not know how to pray as we ought, but the Spirit himself intercedes for us with sighs too deep for words.*
>
> Romans 8:26

Sometimes we just don't know how to pray, either for our patients or for ourselves. Words fail.

In the hospitals where we work there's rarely time to even think, let alone sit down by the bedside and pray with the person whose catheter is clogged, who needs a fresh bandage on a wound or is overdue for their evening antibiotic.

We know what we need for ourselves in those situations, or think we do. Time would be nice—and wisdom. Another pair of hands would be helpful or an administration more responsive to staffing shortages. Better rapport with the physicians would be good, and so would a few less orders. These are the times when it's good to remember Romans and to get better acquainted with the Holy Spirit.

I know I should pray to the Father in the name of Jesus. Often I do. Less often do I stop to remember that it's in the times of my greatest need, the times when I don't know how to pray or even have the time to pray other than a quick "Help me, Lord," that someone else is praying for me. The Spirit helps me in my weakness.

"Likewise the Spirit helps us in our weakness…" It's not a superficial prayer he prays, this Spirit. It's prayers for me with sighs for me—sighs too deep for words.

For me a sigh is often a deep and audible breath I take at the end of a long day at work. A sigh is my expression of fatigue after working a double shift. For the Spirit, though, a sigh is more. His sighs for me are all wrapped up with longing, sorrow, yearning and sometimes with lament. I know those feelings, on the job and in my own personal life at home. They're often hard to express in words. I'm glad the Spirit prays.

It's good to come to God at times and say I don't know what to pray. I just know what I feel and trust the Spirit to interpret what I really need to the Father for myself and others, filtered through His own wise counsel.

Jesus told his disciples he would send them a Counselor, one, I think, with listening skills and a special gift of prayer. "For we do not know how to pray as we ought," wrote Paul.

Today or tonight at work when things get hectic, or at home if that's your busiest time, acknowledge the presence of your wise and ever-present Counselor. Thank him for knowing your heart and being there to pray for you and sigh for you—strong in his strength and in your weakness.

Seek Wisdom

> *And God gave Solomon wisdom and understanding beyond measure, and largeness of mind like the sand on the seashore…*
>
> 1 Kings 4:29

Depression hit like a brick, and my tears of frustration flowed. My dissertation was *not* coming together, and the deadline for completing Chapter 4 was looming.

The first days of spring finally broke through my depression and called me away from the computer. I laced up my walking shoes, pulled on my fleece jacket and set out.

Heading out the door I met Miriam, another graduate student in nursing. We walked and talked about school. Would either of us ever finish? Then Miriam helped me change my perspective.

"I have a friend," she said, "who told me to make a list on one side of the paper of all the things I needed. On the other side she told me to make a list of all the things God was that could meet those needs. So I did. You should try that." I went back to the house and started to make my list. It was a short list. Only one word came to mind. Wisdom.

Psalms began to run through my mind as I began to ask God to give me that thing that seemed to so elude me. "My mouth shall speak wisdom," sings the Psalmist in Psalm 49:3, and "the meditation of my heart shall be understanding."

Lord, I prayed. Give me your understanding. Let understanding be the meditation of my heart.

"The fear of the Lord is the beginning of wisdom," the Psalmist sings in Psalm 111:10 and "a good understanding have all those who practice it."

"Lord," I prayed, "help me to fear you as I should."

I kept going through the Psalms, cross-referencing to

other passages and to other books of the Bible. Proverbs 9:10 echoes the same theme as Psalm 111:10 and ends with the thought that "the knowledge of the Holy One is insight." Wisdom, not in myself but in God.

"Lord, give me knowledge of who you are that my wisdom might also be insightful."

Then I moved to the Gospels and Jesus' promise to the people who would follow him. One day they would be faced with earthquakes, famine, pestilence, terrors and persecution. Jesus knew, I thought, about deadlines and dissertation committees! So what does he say to do? "…I will give you a mouth and wisdom, which none of your adversaries will be able to withstand or contradict" (Luke 21:15). I could trust Jesus for wisdom, granted when I needed it. I had visions of my dissertation defense!

Solomon, the Bible tells us, also had wisdom. When God asked Solomon what he wanted, Solomon asked for wisdom and knowledge to do the work God had called him to do. "Give me now wisdom and knowledge to go out and come in before this people," asks Solomon of God, "for who can rule this thy people, that is so great?" (2 Chronicles 1:10). God gave wisdom and was delighted to do so, simply because he was asked.

I went back to my computer and met my deadline.

What words are on your list today?

Code Blue

> *Trust in the Lord with all your heart, and do not rely on your own insight.*
>
> Proverbs 3:5

I worked the night shift my first year as a nurse and remember it well. "Doing time" was the phrase the older nurses used for it, and it certainly felt like it to me. I started working on a medical-surgical unit and soon switched to intensive care. I was, I thought, filled with faith or presumption, I wasn't sure which. Training for the latter job was minimal.

When my older colleagues were around me, I felt relatively confident. If I got in trouble with a patient, I knew I could always yell and someone would come to my rescue. It was the twenty-minute breaks in the research intensive-care unit that bothered me. Those twenty-minute periods seemed like twenty hours to me, when I needed to relieve the more experienced nurse on duty.

My task seemed easy enough. There was usually no direct patient care. I needed to simply sit and watch the monitors. So I sat and watched and prayed fervently for no straight lines or arrhythmias. It was not a high point of faith in my life. I felt inadequate and unsure of myself and prayed primarily that I'd be able to cope.

When the first code blue did occur in the research intensive-care unit, I did cope. Adrenaline kicks in at times like that, and you find yourself experiencing a renewed surge of energy and power. Remembering what to actually do in that situation, though, I had to attribute to God. With little experience behind me, I could not rely on my own insight. Unsure of myself, I became increasingly sure of God.

Since those early days in nursing there have been many code blue situations in my life, both personally and professionally. I try to think of them as "spiritual emergencies," or situations of crisis that test my faith and ability to trust that God will see me through. My tendency, now that I am older, is to want to simply draw from my own past experiences of coping, but God says his way is better. "In all your ways acknowledge him, and he will make straight your paths," the proverb concludes. (Proverbs 3:6).

Lord, help me today to be more aware of those code blue situations in my life where I am trying to go it alone, relying solely on my own insight instead of yours, or basing my present decisions solely on past experience rather than consulting you in the present. Straighten out my crooked ways of thinking as I place, again, my trust in you.

The Storm Before the Calm

> *And he awoke and rebuked the wind, and said to the sea, "Peace! Be still!" And the wind ceased, and there was a great calm.*
>
> Mark 4:39

When Jesus said to his disciples, "Let us go across to the other side" (Mark 4:35), he didn't tell them the rest of the story. If he had, they might never have climbed in the boat.

Waiting for them on the other side of the sea was a naked man with an unclean spirit, who lived among the tombs. Night and day the man cried out, bruising himself with stones. He was possessed, it seemed, of many demons, enough to cause two thousand swine to plunge to their death in the sea after Jesus cast the spirit out of the man and into the herd of unclean animals. The end result was a man set free and clothed and in his right mind, witnessing to others about what the Lord had done for him.

It doesn't seem surprising that the boat the disciples stepped in would be rocked by waves and threaten to capsize in the storm that rose before the final calm as they journeyed to the land of the tombs. Storms are fitting metaphors for the spiritual battles that need to be fought in our own lives and frequently for others.

For the disciples the battle was for faith and courage in the face of fear. Did they trust Jesus enough to be calm in the midst of what they perceived as danger?

History shows they didn't. They woke Jesus up from a well deserved nap and asked him a rather foolish question. "Teacher," they said, "do you not care if we perish?" (Mark 4:38). Had the thought occurred to them that if *they* perished,

Jesus surely would too? After all, he was the one in the stern, asleep on a cushion.

Jesus may be asking you to get in the boat today and go to the other side. What's on the other side will differ for each of us. It may be a difficult situation at work or a home-life problem you've been reluctant to deal with because of fear. Getting in the boat can mean many things. Confronting instead of avoiding an angry colleague or supervisor. Talking to a patient about the Lord and offering to pray. Dealing with whatever spirits of dysfunction are threatening your personal relationships at home. The story about the storm is a story about healing and obedience.

When you do get in the boat today or some time this week, sailing may not be smooth. But you need to keep in mind the man in the tombs. Remember that Jesus offers freedom. The one who casts out demons can also cause your winds to cease and calm your sea, ensuring you a safe, though not necessarily a trouble-free, passage. All he asks of you is faith to believe he is in control. Faith instead of fear. "Peace! Be still!"

Issues of Blood

For she said, "If I touch even his garments, I shall be made well."

Mark 5:28

In the gospels we find that Jesus was distracted by a woman. Mark describes her being jostled by the crowd following Jesus to the home of Jairus, an important ruler of the synagogue whose daughter was terminally ill.

Put yourself in this situation. You are that woman or perhaps you're a man with a twelve-year-old "issue of blood." You've gone to countless physicians or counselors. You've suffered much and wasted more and spent all your meager savings on worthless remedy after worthless remedy, traditional and alternative. Your condition has only gotten worse, sapping your strength, wearing you down. Your twelve-year-old bleeding condition must surely seem insignificant, you think, compared to the impending death of a twelve-year-old child, but twelve years seems a terribly long time to wait.

But you've heard stories. One was about a paralytic man who was lowered through the roof by four of his friends. He landed at the feet of Jesus and was healed. You've also heard a rumor about a man with a withered hand who stretched it out to Jesus and received it back straight and strong, and about a naked demoniac who lived in the tombs, who encountered Jesus and was now free from a spirit of destruction; he's now clothed and in his right mind.

This Jesus is a teacher, a Jew, a holy man of God. You, in contrast, are an ordinary man or woman with a bleeding condition; you're considered unclean. How can you possibly think you could approach, much less touch, a person like him? But you remember the men who lowered their paralyzed friend through the roof. You remember the man who reached out to touch Jesus with his withered hand. Even the man who was demon possessed ran up to Jesus, knowing instinctively he would not be turned away.

Close your eyes and visualize the scene. Come to the scene with your senses. As you identify with this woman, what are you thinking and feeling? What is your own issue of blood, your own chronic long-term condition in need of healing? What do you want to say to Jesus? What do you want him to do for you? Then go ahead. Be brave. Reach out with your faith, even if you think it's small. You don't need much. Even a brief encounter with the hem of Jesus' garments will do.

Power went out of Jesus when the woman with the issue of blood touched him and he, in turn, was touched with her infirmity. Power went out of him and into her, making her *feel* healed as well as *be* healed. Her chronic bleeding condition dried up.

"Daughter. Your faith has made you well; go in peace, and be healed of your disease." Hear Jesus speaking to you today.

Desolate Pits and Miry Bogs

> *He drew me up from the desolate pit, out of the miry bog, and set my feet upon a rock, making my steps secure.*

Psalm 40:2

A recent conversation with a friend made the present-day reality of cost containment very clear. She shared with me her loss of a job as a nurse in an intensive-care unit of a large teaching hospital in the wake of budget cuts. "I'm sinking fast," she said, reflecting on her loss of income and unpaid bills.

Sinking fast. The writer of Psalm 40 paints a vivid picture of a person who has fallen into a bog or pit of quicksand and is sinking fast. When the ground seems exceedingly soggy, the mud deep, and you've fallen in up to your neck, the natural tendency is to panic. The human response is to struggle, to fight, to try and claw your way to the surface, out to dry land. Yet struggling, fighting and clawing is the last thing to do if you want to survive. What may be needed most if you've fallen into a miry bog is the ability to stay calm and relaxed. You also need to cry out to be rescued. Not crying out in the first place because of embarrassment about falling into the pit is, in fact, a prescription for disaster.

Today as I reread Psalm 40 I think of the desolate pits and miry bogs of my own life I have fallen into, often of my own making. I usually struggled to try and extricate myself. Sometimes my struggles paid off, but often the emotional and physical toll was high. Other times I rested more, realizing my inability to save myself and my need, like the Psalmist's, to finally reach up and grasp another's arm. When the Psalmist did that God pulled him up, out of the mud and mire, and set him down again, gently but firmly, on a solid place, with a gentle reminder, I suspect, to stay there.

Psalm 40 reminds me to steer clear of the miry bogs, but it also reminds me to praise the Lord for his rescues when my foot has slipped. The end result of my deliverance may be the salvation of others. "Many will see and fear and put their trust in the Lord," writes the Psalmist after being rescued himself (Psalm 40:3). Amazing!

My desolate pits and miry bog experiences can become the means for bringing others closer to the Lord as they see his ability to rescue in times of trouble, as I tell others about my deliverance and of God's saving mercy.

Telling others of our desolate pit experiences can be painful and humbling as we reveal our own human frailties and foibles, but that is what we're encouraged to do. "He put a new song in my mouth, a song of praise to our God," wrote the Psalmist (v. 3). Sing some songs today as you reflect on your own experiences of rescue in times of trouble.

To a Lonely Place

> *And he said to them, "Come away by yourselves to a lonely place, and rest awhile." For many were coming and going, and they had no leisure even to eat.*

Mark 6:31

"Everything seems to be unraveling," my friend Joan said to me last week. Work was stressful. A hospice nurse, Joan was filling in for a sick co-worker and caring for six clients, all of whom were at death's door.

Tonight I called another friend who works in community health. She had just returned from a thirteen-hour shift. Six charts were on her kitchen table to complete before morning. The day before, theoretically, had been a well-deserved day off, but an elderly neighbor called her, complaining of chest pains, and Jane had spent most of the day and half the night in the hospital with her. The holiday weekend coming up was rapidly filling with visits she needed to make as the only on-call nurse for her agency.

"I feel," Jane said, "a little bit weary."

Relief from weariness to prevent unraveling is something most nurses need. Jesus' words to his disciples, "Come away by yourselves to a lonely place, and rest awhile," strike a responsive chord. If we only could, we think, we would.

The early disciples also faced this problem. Their job description was similar to ours. Jesus had recruited them, then sent them out into the community to preach the good news of the kingdom but also to heal the sick, the few caring for the many.

After one particularly successful venture in physical and spiritual health care, the disciples came back to Jesus, weary, I suspect, from all their work but also pumped up with enthusiasm at the positive response to their caregiving ministry: people repented, demons departed, the sick got well.

I picture Jesus listening patiently to their stories. But he also knew their real need was to come apart, rest awhile and nourish their physical bodies before they literally unraveled and came apart.

Like busy hospice or community health nurses, I picture the disciples scarfing down a quick loaf of bread or a bunch of grapes or figs on the run while dashing off to the next visit to meet yet another person's needs. Jesus tells them to stop. The work will be there when they get back. Come away. Eat a good meal. Rest awhile.

The place Jesus urged the disciples to come away to was a lonely place. So far, so good, but their break was short lived. Crowds followed them, even to the lonely place. Yet it was there, in that lonely place, that Jesus did one of his greatest miracles. He multiplied the loaves and fishes and fed the crowds. He also fed his disciples and met their physical need for rest and refreshment.

This week or next, if everything seems to be unraveling and you find yourself a little bit weary, take some extra time to come apart to a lonely place to be with Jesus. Jesus fed the five thousand; he also fed the twelve, strengthening them to return to ministry, revealing his power to them—in the lonely place.

The Med Error

But who can discern his errors? Clear thou me from hidden faults.

Psalm 19:12

Wrong patient, wrong pill, wrong dosage, allergic reaction. The patient survived, but the nurse wasn't sure he would.

Nursing is stressful. Medication errors are made. None of us is immune, from the student in nursing to the most experienced nurse. When we make those errors our hearts sink, our hands shake, our skin gets cold and clammy and our minds are filled with visions of lawsuits. We may even cover up the error by not reporting it, particularly if there are no obvious side effects noted. Or we may wrestle with the idea of covering it up, then feel guilty about entertaining the thought.

David knew a lot about errors in judgment; he made many of them. He was also well acquainted with the rule book for preventing and dealing with errors once made. In Psalm 19 he reminds himself and us that the law of the Lord is perfect and the testimony of the Lord sure (v. 7). He goes on to say that the precepts of the Lord are right, the commandments pure and the ordinances true and righteous (vv. 8–9). The written Word gave him instruction for living, even to the smallest details of his life and work, and was intended to be obeyed and sought after. More to be desired are they than gold, David argues, comparing the words of the Lord to honey and the drippings of the honeycomb (v. 10).

Christian nurses can echo the words of David. Yet even with the written Word and the witness of the Holy Spirit in our hearts, revealing truth to us and giving us discernment about right from wrong, we still make errors. We have momentary lapses in judgment in nursing that can cause us and others distress. We can also be guilty of "hidden faults," areas of our lives that need correction and reorientation that others may be aware of but we may deny or remain ignorant of. And, too, there is the "presumptuous sin" and "transgression"—that deliberate and willful disobedience that threatens to gain dominion as our flesh wages war with our spirits.

Wrong patient, wrong pill, wrong dosage, allergic reaction. As long as we remain in nursing we are going to be subject to med errors. As long as we remain human we are going to be subject to many other errors, to lapses in judgment, hidden faults, to secret and presumptuous sin. Thankfully, like David, we have a God who knows our frames and who delights that we come to him daily, asking for his help in responding to all the "med errors" of our life.

Lord, today in my nursing and in my life apart from my workaday world, help me discern my errors; reveal them to me and clear me from any hidden faults. Help me resist the temptation to commit presumptuous sin. Let the meditations of my heart be pleasing to you, and the words of my mouth acceptable.

Unblushing Persistence and Incessant Appeals

> *I tell you, though he will not get up and give him anything because he is his friend, yet because of his importunity he will rise and give him whatever he needs.*
>
> Luke 11:8

In the Parish Nurse courses I have taught, the role of an *advocate* always surfaced when I asked nurses how they defined what they did. An advocate is someone who pleads another's cause verbally or in writing, usually to a higher authority who is in the position to provide what that person needs.

What people did you care for this week who needed an advocate? Was it someone like Mildred Smith who was discharged from the orthopedic unit on the weekend but is not yet capable of safely transferring from her bed to the chair or navigating the route from her bedroom to her bathroom and refuses to use a commode? What do you do when Mildred's neighbor calls you and asks for your help? What resources can be mobilized in the middle of the night to help this eighty-eight-year-old woman in your congregation who slipped through the cracks of discharge planning?

Being an advocate in nursing requires we do our homework by becoming aware of community and congregational resources to help people like Mildred in the middle of the night. Being advocates as Christian nurses also requires we do our homework by becoming aware of biblical role models for us to give us vision and encouragement.

One role model is the advocate in Luke 11 whose hungry friend came to him at midnight. What did this advocate do? He went to another friend, knocked on his door, and told him his need. But he didn't just ask, he importuned. To importune is to trouble with requests or demands, to urge or repeatedly persist. *Unblushing persistence* is the way one commentary defines importunity. I like that phrase. It gives me courage.

Luke 11 is, in fact, all about advocacy. As the chapter opens, we see Jesus in prayer, advocating, we might assume, for the world he came to serve and save. When his disciples ask him to teach them to pray, he shares with them the familiar Lord's Prayer, couched in the context of the theme of advocacy, friends pleading for the needs of their friends, parents pleading for the needs of their children.

Luke 18 paints yet another portrait of importunity. A widow functions as her own advocate, coming before the judge to demand vindication from a troublesome adversary. The woman receives what she wants and needs, not simply because she asked, but because of her persistence. "She will wear me out by her continual coming" is the phrase used by the judge who will grant her request (Luke 18:5). *Incessant appealing* is the way another commentary on Luke defines it. I like that.

It makes me bold.

Lord, make me aware this week of people you put in my path who need an advocate. Help me be aware of my own limitations, but help me be more aware of other resources available to help meet needs. Let me be unblushingly persistent and incessantly appealing with you as I advocate for myself and others.

The Waiting Room

The Waiting Room

> *Therefore the Lord waits to be gracious to you; therefore he exalts himself to show mercy to you. For the Lord is a God of justice; blessed are all those who wait for him.*
>
> Isaiah 30:18

We all know that hospitals have them. They're called waiting rooms. Sometimes they're small areas designed for families waiting to see loved ones in intensive-care units, where time for visits is often limited to five-minute or ten-minute intervals every two hours. Sometimes they are large congregate areas where friends and relatives gather, waiting for loved ones to come out of surgery. People spend a lot of time in waiting rooms.

Waiting for news of a loved one is never easy. The old adage, "Time marches on" seems not to apply to these seemingly interminable situations of waiting for good news or bad. Minutes go by like hours, hours like days. The score seems marked to be played largo. We want it to be presto. Checking the clock on the wall and pacing around the room are the main activities of people in hospital waiting rooms.

Waiting for God to answer our prayers is a lot like being a relative or friend in a waiting room. This is especially true when we have a concern for a loved one or for ourselves that, to us, seems extremely urgent and in need of God's immediate attention and action. We bring our petitions and supplications to God in prayer, but then we're often forced to wait. God usually sends us, in fact, directly to the waiting room, not to the surgical suite. Go, he says, and wait. Trust me. I know what I'm doing. This isn't my first operation.

We go to the waiting room reluctantly, constantly checking the clock on the wall and restlessly pacing the halls. If we only had a cell phone, we'd call up God directly and ask what was taking so long. Instead, we worry. It gives us something to do. Why aren't our prayers answered now? Isn't God aware of how desperate we are? Doesn't he know we're on a deadline here?

The people of God have always had trouble waiting. This was true of the Israelites. Their tendency was to run ahead and "speed upon horses." God was constantly reminding them there was a better way. He encouraged them to reflect on their history. Whenever enemies were pursuing them, the Israelites tended to run. God's advice was always different. Stand still. Trust. Wait. Don't be concerned with the time. "In returning and rest you shall be saved; in quietness and in trust shall be your strength" (Isaiah 30:15–16).

God, too, has spent a considerable amount of time in waiting rooms. He has always patiently waited to be gracious to his people, waited for them to trust. He waits for us, too, to stop our frantic pacing and our clock-watching. He waits for us to return and rest in him. Isaiah reminds us that our patiently waiting God also has a good and perfect plan for our lives that includes showering us with mercy. He is, says Isaiah, a "God of justice," and "blessed are all those who wait for him" (Isaiah 30:18). Lord, teach me today to patiently wait for you.

The Land of the Living

> *I believe that I shall see the goodness of the Lord in the land of the living! Wait for the Lord; be strong, and let your heart take courage; yea, wait for the Lord!*

Psalm 27:13–14

Most of the people we care for are in pain; many are dying. For Christians in pain or dying, glimpses of heaven can remind them that true goodness of body waits in a realm called eternal life, but they may have difficulty seeing God's goodness for them in the present.

The Psalmist, though, was not content with only a futuristic hope. Goodness was a reality to be grasped today. The Psalmist had a very present desire to see the goodness of God in the land of the living.

I am encouraged by people in crisis who populate the Old Testament books. They were honest folk who rarely hid their feelings. One of my home-care clients, a Christian man, age ninety-eight, described them best to me. They were not, he said, "super-duper holy."

Not being super-duper holy means we can be honest with God and encourage our patients to be so, too. That's often comforting to people in pain who feel they should never be angry with God or question the meaning of goodness.

"Do the shades rise up to praise thee? Is thy steadfast love declared in the grave…?" The Psalmist's cry is a call for help, rising out of a soul that is full of troubles. Close to death, from his "youth up," the Psalmist suffers "terrors" and considers himself "helpless" (Psalm 88:10–11, 15). Sometimes when I read this Psalm, I am tempted to say to the Psalmist, "Get a grip." He seems to have an exaggerated sense of his doom and gloom. But he was, I note, nothing if not honest about his feelings.

Job, the Old Testament figure who certainly seemed to have the most legitimate cause for complaints, after losing his health, his wealth and all his children in one fell swoop, complains to God about his plight; yet he also clings to the hope that he will experience God's goodness in the present life, not only in the hereafter. Job's faith in the midst of adverse circumstances seems to echo the words of Isaiah: "From of old no one has heard or perceived by the ear, no eye has seen a God besides thee, who works for those who wait for him" (Isaiah 64:4).

Psalm 27 in particular seems to be an acknowledgment, a statement, of faith. It's an affirmation and challenge we need to take seriously for ourselves. "I believe that I shall see the goodness of the Lord in the land of living! Wait for the Lord; be strong, and let your heart take courage; yea, wait for the Lord" (Psalm 27:13–14).

The Psalmist knew an important truth. As bad as the circumstances looked, God had not abandoned him. Though complete wholeness in physical body might come in the form of a resurrected one, God's goodness in the midst of pain and suffering is a present, not a future hope.

Lord, help me know your present goodness in my own daily life in the face of adverse circumstances, and help me communicate this truth to those I daily care for who are in pain and dying.

God in the Wilderness

The wilderness and the dry land shall be glad, the desert shall rejoice and blossom.

Isaiah 35:1

I remember one winter vacation I took years ago when I was particularly burned out in nursing and grieving over the personal loss of a relationship. I hiked a portion of the Appalachian Trail. "Uninhabited, uncultivated, waste and wild"; according to the dictionary definition, the trail fit the description of a wilderness.

Personal wilderness experiences are not uncommon for nurses, and they're certainly not uncommon for people nurses care for. Sickness, suffering, sin and any number of other circumstances can bring us to the wilderness, to the waste and wild and lonely places.

Hagar, the woman who bore Ishmael, Abraham's son, was driven into the wilderness by Sarah (Genesis 21).

Because of their rebellion and murmuring against the Lord who brought them out of the bondage of Egypt, the Israelites were brought by God into the wilderness, where they faced forty years of wilderness wandering (Numbers 14; Ezekiel 20:8–10).

David spent a considerable amount of time in the wilderness, running and hiding from King Saul (1 Samuel 26:1–3).

Jesus faced forty days and forty nights in the wilderness, driven there by the Spirit and tempted there by Satan (Matthew 4:1–2).

But for Hagar, the Israelites, David and Jesus, their wilderness had a flip side.

It was in the wilderness Hagar received the promise for Ishmael, her son, whose descendants would greatly multiply.

She saw God as the "God of seeing" and believed (Genesis 16:13) and the "God who hears" who rescued and gives hope (Genesis 21:17).

It was in the "great and terrible wilderness, with its fiery serpents and scorpions and thirsty ground where there was no water" that God brought water out of the rock and fed his rebellious people with manna (Deuteronomy. 8:15–16). There in the wilderness, the Israelites knew the meaning of the Lord as provider.

In the wilderness of Ziph, where David refrained from killing a sleeping, vulnerable Saul, he learned the meaning of the mercy of the Lord (1 Samuel 26:9–12).

In the Galilean wilderness Jesus experienced the full power of the enemy unleashed. He learned the meaning of relying on his Father's strength to resist the wiles of the enemy and was ministered to by angels (Matthew 4:1–11).

Hiking the Appalachian Trail in winter, I experienced God as restorer of both my soul and my perspective.

"The wilderness and the dry land shall be glad, the desert shall rejoice and blossom; like the crocus it shall blossom abundantly and rejoice with joy and singing...and sorrow and sighing shall flee away" (Isaiah 35:1–2, 10).

Sometimes we are forced to go into the wilderness by sickness, accident, or impending death. Sometimes God leads us there for other reasons. One thing we can cling to in our wilderness experience is that we are not alone, and the experience itself does not have to be unfruitful, barren, waste —for in the wilderness is God.

Do You Want to Be Healed?

"Do you want to be healed?"

John 5:6

I've often wondered why Jesus asked the man the question, "Do you want to be healed?" After all, he had been ill, Scripture tells us, for thirty-eight years.

The pool the man was lying by called Beth-zatha was an interesting place. The area around the pool was an infirmary of sorts with five porticoes. People were waiting there—blind and lame and paralyzed, victims, perhaps, of chronic diabetes, arthritis and strokes. They needed long-term care or healing. And then there was the man lying on his pallet. We don't know what his ailment was but Jesus did.

The pool was a place of healing, supernaturally so. An angel was involved, sent by God at certain times and certain seasons to stir up and trouble the water to somehow effect a cure for those who entered in.

Thirty-eight years was a long time, I think, to wait for healing. The man's first response to Jesus' question, "Do you want to be healed?" was "Sir, I have no man to put me into the pool when the water is troubled." But then he said, "While I am going another steps down before me" (v. 7). Others appeared to beat him to it; he made the effort, hesitated, and all was lost. His story lacks consistency.

Jesus asks me the same question. He knows I, too, need healing from my own "long-term illnesses," not my physical ailments, but my secret, chronic sins and long-term habits. My stories, too, have lacked consistency. I've made excuses. I've blamed others for my lack of healing or my own inability to change. I've blamed myself that others have what I want or get what I lack. I've made the effort, hesitated.

But Jesus sees my need. He knows my situation. He bids me rise. Take up my pallet. Walk.

We read in John the man was healed.

When he stopped making excuses.

When he stopped blaming himself.

When he stopped blaming others.

When he simply recognized his need and rose.

Obedience was his answer to Jesus' question. Finally. Healing. After thirty-eight years.

Lord, today I come again to you for healing. You know my need. You know the excuses I've given over the years that prevented me from changing. Help me be obedient to your voice simply calling me to obey you. Lord, today I would rise, take up my pallet, walk. I want to be healed.

Perfect Timing

But when the time had fully come, God sent forth his Son…

Galatians 4:4

In his devotional guide *Come Before Winter and Share My Hope*, Charles Swindoll reflects on Galatians 4:4 and the "perfectly synchronized events" surrounding Jesus' birth two thousand years ago.*

Those events included a "bothersome census" decreed by Rome that forced a very pregnant mother-to-be from Galilee to journey to Judah to deliver a child, as prophesied hundreds of years before by a man named Micah. When the time had fully come, Jesus was born, not sooner, not later, but according to God's perfect plan.

That phrase, "when the time had fully come" is a good one to ponder in relation to our own goals and objectives. I've always been good at developing rather elaborate ones in my life, but generally unrealistic about the time frame needed to accomplish them. Discouraged by what I perceive as (and what often *is*) my own lack of discipline, it's sometimes easier to give up than to keep trying and striving and believing that "in the fullness of time," if I do my part, God will do his.

The preacher in Ecclesiastes 3 reminds us, too, that for everything there is a season, for birth and death, planting and harvest, mourning and dancing, casting away and gathering. There is a time and a place for every matter under heaven, including the fulfillment of hopes and dreams, goals and objectives. That time is God's appointed time.

Knowing that God is ultimately in control of all the details of my life does not eliminate my free will. I still have my job to do, and at times I may fail to do it and fail, in my own estimation, miserably. In my failures, though, I need to remember that all things work together for good, and God can take my failures and mistakes and weave them into a meaningful pattern where nothing in my life is wasted.

In Galatians, a contrast is set up between slaves and children. Slaves, Paul notes, had no essential rights to property; children did though these children and heirs needed to grow up and be of a certain age to legally inherit and possess their inheritance. The child had to wait for the father's blessing, wait until the appointed time.

What "inheritance" are you waiting for today? What goals and objectives need accomplishing? What hopes and dreams do you want to see fulfilled? To appreciate God's present and future timetable more, reflect back to hopes realized, dreams fulfilled and goals and objectives accomplished both personally and professionally in your past. Remember and thank God for his perfect timing in orchestrating events and working out his purposes in those situations for your best good.

Lord, today in my own anxious moments about my future and in the face of yet-to-be-accomplished goals and objectives, give me the faith to believe you are working behind the scenes of my life to accomplish your purposes in me and for me for my own best good. Help me to live all of life believing and resting in the fullness of time.

*Charles R. Swindoll. *Come Before Winter and Share My Hope*. (Tyndale House Publishers, Inc., 1997).

I'm Normal!

For everything there is a season, and a time for every matter under heaven.

Ecclesiastes 3:1

His wife had died six months before, and I was visiting again, this time helping him plant his garden—row after row of potatoes, squash and peas. When we finally finished, Mr. Case invited me in for a glass of iced tea. We sat in silence. He never did much talking on my visits but always seemed to like the company.

I sensed, though, he really needed to talk about his wife's death. It was a subject he always avoided. "I'm OK," was all he'd ever say at church when anyone asked him. "I'm doing fine." His initial response the day of my visit had been the same.

When I was ready to leave I offered him a book on grief, thinking he might refuse or be offended. "I think you should read this," I said, hesitantly.

He glared at me for a minute and shook his head as if he was about to say no, but he took the book. A few days later I received a phone call. Mr. Case was shouting on the other end of the line. "I'm normal! I'm normal! I'm normal!"

Sometimes people we care for as nurses in our congregations or other settings need a little help from others to get in touch with their feelings. Grief work is tough and admitting to feelings of anger or depression, hard. The guilt that frequently is associated with feelings and thoughts is normal, too, but even harder to admit to or express. Bibliotherapy can help them as we loan them books like Granger Westberg's *Good Grief** or testimonies of personal experience like C.S. Lewis' *A Grief Observed.***

The Psalms are also a rich repository of feelings expressed. Their writers remind us that though grief work is hard, it's also a needed and normal response to abnormal situations. That abnormal situation can be the death of a relative or close friend or maybe the death of a dream. All losses require grief. In the Psalms, David vented his anger. He bargained with God and was depressed. His emotions ran the gamut of the crisis cycle so familiar to us in nursing. Similar emotions rise up and spill over in Psalms written by others.

Going through grief is usually a long slow process, a little like planting a garden and waiting for it to grow. Our tears may fall like seeds sown on dry and fallow ground, and we wonder, as we're going through the grief, will there ever be an end to it? Will there ever be another harvest of growing things in our lives?

God says yes. For everything there is a season, a time for every matter under heaven (Ecclesiastes 3:1). Birth and death, weeping and laughing, mourning and dancing, planting and plucking up.

If people you care for in nursing are having trouble getting in touch with their feelings, introduce them through bibliotherapy to others who have walked a similar path—going through grief work, weeping yet waiting for the harvest.

*Granger E. Westberg. *Good Grief.* (Augsburg Fortress Publishers, 1979).

**C.S. Lewis. *A Grief Observed.* (Seabury Press, 1961).

Labor

> *Therefore, my beloved brethren, be steadfast, immovable, always abounding in the work of the Lord, knowing that in the Lord your labor is not in vain.*

1 Corinthians 15:58

Labor and delivery. Some of you work there now, and all of us have had some experience of it, at some point in our nursing careers, if it only meant standing huddled with our fellow nursing students at the foot of the delivery table, watching with awe the birth of a baby as we listened to the doctor yell, "Push!"

The process of giving birth to a baby is one of those things that are believed to be "not in vain." It's not futile striving. It's not a fruitless activity but a fruitful one. It's not a worthless effort but an effort shot through with value and significance.

Delivery also prompts images of abounding. A woman, immediately after delivery, as her newborn is placed on her breast, is an image of abounding in her work, fully abounding in joy. The word *abound*, literally, means "to rise in waves," like a land overflowing with grain.

Your labor is not in vain. Mothers-to-be may need to be reminded of that by nurses in the difficult stages of labor. They have to stay the course, concentrate on breathing, focus on the ultimate goal, refuse to give up. Delivery will come eventually, and soon the pain of labor will be worth all the effort spent in waiting and in working.

Our labor is not in vain. Reflect today on areas of your life in nursing or in your personal life where you feel your striving is in vain. Ask God to give you a greater vision of the goals toward which you've been working personally or professionally. For the mother-to-be, the goal is a child. For the

Corinthians, it was a resurrection body that many in the church had lost sight of, with disastrous consequences for the way they chose to live their lives in the present. They stopped striving, stopped working, stopped believing in the goal.

Lord, keep me focused on the good goals you have for me personally and professionally; help me stay focused on those goals, believing that the work I do to make them a reality is not work done in vain, but will eventually bring forth fruit, at the appointed time.

And Delivery

> *I sought the Lord, and he answered me, and delivered me from all my fears.*
>
> Psalm 34:4

"Call us if you need us," I remember the anesthesiologist saying as she was donning her sterile cap and gown for her tour of duty in the OR. "You'll be fine," said the surgeon, also slipping into sterile greens.

While meant to reassure, their words were less than comforting. I sincerely doubted whether any complication I might encounter as the nurse in charge of delivering babies would win out over major abdominal surgery; the words of the anesthesiologist and surgeon rang a bit hollow to me. I hoped and prayed I wouldn't have to test my theory.

My method for delivering babies would probably not have instilled a whole lot of confidence in the mothers-to-be or my former nursing instructors, had they known that at the bottom of the delivery table my nursing textbook was open to a chapter titled "Obstetric Complications." My short-term stint as a summer missionary nurse in Ethiopia had become a crash course in labor and delivery. My prayer was that these women would know God as their deliverer and that I would be faithful in cooperating with this venture, hopefully with no complications.

The theme of being delivered runs throughout Scripture from Genesis to Revelation. The Psalmist is constantly asking God to deliver him: from his enemies (Psalm 59:1), from troubles (Psalm 34:6), from sin (Psalm 51:1–2), from the emotional and physical storms of life (Psalm 18:16–19) and even from death (Psalm 6:4). These deliveries were complicated, not easy. The enemies, the troubles, the sin, the emotional and physical storms and the threat of impending death were only too real. He named and acknowledged his fears in the present and the future and trusted in God's ability to deliver him.

What do you need to be delivered from today? Call on God if you need him, then hear him say to you, "Daughter, I am with you. Son, I am with you. You really will be fine."

Listening Ears and Laundry Detergent

> *When the crowds learned it, they followed him; and he welcomed them and spoke to them of the kingdom of God, and cured those who had need of healing.*
>
> Luke 9:11

A number of years ago I received a letter from my friend, Anne. She wrote the following: "I spent the day with a friend who needed to get away from the noise and busyness of the infirmary where she has been working as a camp nurse for the summer. She needed to do her laundry. My own nursing skills are pretty rusty but perhaps this is my *own* style of camp ministry; I can provide for her a warm welcome, peace, quiet, rest, a listening ear— and laundry detergent."

Sometimes it's we ourselves who need to be nursed, as Anne acknowledged in her letter to me, reflecting on her own "rusty skills" but also well aware of the needs of active duty nurses. To my mind, Anne is also doing active duty nursing. A warm welcome, peace, quiet, rest and a listening ear are all elements of nursing that sometimes get neglected in the health care systems we're a part of. We want them to characterize our lives as we care for others, but the demands of the job often reflect environments characterized, instead, by depersonalization.

Warm welcomes characterized Jesus' life and ministry. Before he spoke of the kingdom, before he reached out to heal, he reached out to welcome the crowds. What did that welcome consist of? Luke doesn't tell us, but we can imagine that it might have included a listening ear and an invitation to come away for some peace, quiet and rest. After he preached to them and cured those in need of healing, Jesus also reached out and offered hospitality—food for their hungry bodies.

Welcome and hospitality also characterized the life of the early church. Without it the gospel would never have spread around the world. The disciples, and later the apostles, were dependent on the hospitality of those who took them in, providing them with lodging, food and a place to unwind after busy days of ministry, a home away from home (see, for example, Matthew 10:1–14; Acts 10:6 and Acts 16:15). Show hospitality to both friends and strangers, Paul tells the early Christians. Some of those strangers might be angels. And some might even be Jesus himself. You never know! "...for I was hungry and you gave me food, I was thirsty and you gave me drink, I was a stranger and you welcomed me…" says Jesus, reflecting on his second coming and the judgment of the nations (Matthew 25:35).

"I can provide for her a warm welcome, peace, quiet, rest, a listening ear—and laundry detergent." The personal touch. My friend's letter challenges me to think about my own responsibilities and what it means to show hospitality to hurting people I care for in the nursing home or hospital or to the students I teach in the classroom. Peace, quiet, rest and the offer of a listening ear. All these are needed by people in pain or by students in need of a home away from home. Thank you, Lord, for the reminder that one of the most important things we can do in nursing is welcome.

Running on Empty

Running on Empty

Arise and eat, else the journey will be too great for you.

1 Kings 19:7

The road home was all downhill. I coasted to a stop about half a mile from the gas station. My father, I thought, would not be pleased. I remembered with a guilty conscience his advice to me when I first started to drive: "Always keep your eye on the gas tank. Never let it get below a quarter full." A community health nurse for several years, I should have learned that lesson well, but here I was again, hiking on the highway as my penalty for running on empty.

Elijah had that problem, too. 1 Kings 18 describes a pretty spectacular confrontation God's prophet had with the prophets of the false god Baal. Full of faith, and also full of presumption, Elijah called on the Lord to prove himself. God honored his prophet's request and sent down fire from heaven. But shortly thereafter we see a fearful Elijah, forgetful of God's power, fleeing for his life. He was running, it would seem, on empty. Alone in the wilderness, Elijah finally sat down under a broom tree and promptly fell asleep, burned out, it appears, by too much ministry. "Take away my life," he says to God. "It is enough" (1 Kings 19:4).

God, however, had other plans for his troubled prophet. He sent an angel and woke Elijah up. "Arise and eat," the angel told the prophet, "else the journey will be too great for you" (v. 7). You've got more work to do, places to go, people to see. Stop complaining. Strengthen your will. Fill up your tank and move on.

Running on empty is a reality nurses in any clinical setting can identify with. Our jobs demand a lot of time and energy, and running is often what we all do best. We spend our days in nursing darting here and there, assessing needs, changing dressings, trying to keep up with a never-ending pile of paperwork. It's all too easy to start on the run and, when the shift is done, find ourselves coasting to a stop with no more time and no more energy left. Running on an empty tank of gas can be a metaphor for our inner state of being spiritually drained.

So what's the solution? Keeping a more watchful eye on my gas gauge is one thing I can do by taking some needed time-outs periodically throughout each day to add to my tank. These might be five-minute prayer breaks, or a few minutes out of each hour to read a verse of Scripture. They may be singing a hymn in my car or using the opportunity between clients to memorize a verse of Scripture I've taped to my dashboard. It also means making a concerted effort to spend more quality time alone with God each day, apart from the workaday world, to fill my tank.

I can easily identify with Elijah. I, too, want to sometimes sit down under a broom tree and fall asleep. When I get that way, I know it's time to check all my gauges and heed the advice the angel gave to his sleeping prophet. I need to arise, eat, fill up my tank and move on.

Bread

> *Jesus said to them, "I am the bread of life; he who comes to me shall not hunger, and he who believes in me shall never thirst."*
>
> John 6:35

It was one in the morning, and I was still tossing and turning, frustrated because I couldn't sleep. Only a few hours and then the Easter sunrise service would begin. For once I wasn't on call at the home-care agency, but I still felt like a night nurse.

Quiet! I wanted to scream. My upstairs neighbors were cooking again, slamming cupboard doors, moving chairs, running the garbage disposal.

Half an hour passed. The noise from the carefree cooks had faded, but I was still wide-awake. It must have been the coffee, I reasoned, or all those hours at the computer typing my dissertation. Worry that I might never finish it. My lack of income, canceled health insurance, unpaid bills. Sleep. I wanted it so I could forget.

Then came the smell, seeping down through the cracks in the ceiling and in through the crack of my window. The smell of fresh-baked bread. In the middle of the night my noisy neighbors were giving me a spiritual lesson. Physical hunger aside, I knew my primary need was for spiritual food. What I needed was to settle down and trust in the Bread of Life.

A few hours later the Easter sunrise service again reminded me of that reality as we shared together, as a congregation, the bread and the wine and experiences of the Lord's involvement in our lives the preceding week.

In John's Gospel I read that the people were seeking Jesus and wanted more. They wanted more food to keep their stomachs full and more of those concrete everyday possessions. But an empty stomach and lack of possessions weren't their problems. The true emptiness and lack were in their souls. Their need was not to feed on fresh-baked bread but to feast on the words of Jesus. Their primary need was not for food that would perish but for food that would endure to eternal life.

Income to pay bills, health insurance, a dissertation to complete. Jesus knows my material needs. He also knows my heart.

Lord, this morning, make me more aware of my true heart hunger, my primary need to hunger and thirst for you. Let me come to you and be satisfied. All the rest can wait.

Familiar Friends

> *"Oh, that I were as in the months of old, as in the days when God watched over me…"*

Job 29:2

He patted me on the arm and motioned for me to come into his room. His speech was a bit garbled, and as he tried to tell me what was agitating him, he became even less coherent. Finally he pointed to the empty bed by the window. His roommate had been taken to the hospital that morning with acute abdominal pain. Tears filled his eyes, and he was able to tell me so I understood. "But he was my pal. He cared about me."

Not all living situations are as close as the one that had been forged by the two men on the nursing-home unit where I worked. The biblical writers, though, speak about similar kinds of friendships.

David, in Psalm 55, reflects on a past relationship with a "familiar friend," with whom he held "sweet converse" and "walked in fellowship" (vv. 13–14). In 1 Samuel we read that Jonathan loved David "as he loved his own soul" (I Samuel 20:17). Jesus speaks about the kind and quality of love that would impel people to lay down their very lives for their friends (John 15:13). Paul's encouragement to "greet one another with a holy kiss" (1 Corinthians 16:20) surely implied the most intimate of friendships among believers.

Yet the greatest friendship of all is the friendship we can have with God. This was a type of friendship very foreign to early Greek culture and to people in today's culture who view God as being far removed from the cares of this world, as distant, unknowable and unapproachable (Acts 17:23). This is not the God Paul knew, who desires to relate very personally to the people he created and in whom we "live and move and have our being" (Acts 17:27–28). An unapproachable God is not the God of the Psalmist who wrote of the "friendship of the Lord" and a personal, knowable God who could relieve both the troubles of his heart and his distress (Psalm 25:14–17).

Friendship with God was especially important to those who were older. Three times we see Abraham identified as the friend of God (2 Chronicles 20:7; Isaiah 41:8; James 2:23). Moses knew the friendship of the Lord as God spoke to him face-to-face, clearly, not in dark speech, but as a friend (Exodus 33:11; Numbers 12:8). Job reflected long on the intimate relationship he had always known with the God who "watched over" him and cared about him in the "autumn" of his days (Job 29:2–4). The memory of God's friendship was made even more acute by Job's present situation of suffering and his current inability to experience that intimacy and emotional attachment he'd once enjoyed. Yet Job knew God was still there, even in the darkness, and he came to the end of his situation of personal suffering, seeing God for himself, no longer content with merely hearing about him from others or having just a casual, taken-for-granted relationship with him (Job 42:5).

Pray today at work for the people of all ages you care for, that in their longings for friendship they may come to truly know the friendship of the Lord and experience sweet converse in the spring, summer, autumn or winter of their lives.

Cramming for Finals

> *Then the kingdom of heaven shall be compared to ten maidens who took their lamps and went to meet the bridegroom. Five of them were foolish, and five were wise.*
>
> Matthew 25:1–2

Where did that question come from? I don't know the answer. Did we ever study that in obstetrics? I'll never pass this test!

Cramming for finals. Students are well acquainted with the signs and symptoms. The night before the exam, all the questions we review are the ones we can't answer. We pull all-nighters and drink bottomless cups of coffee or cans of Coke. We should have studied more and sooner, we reason with hindsight.

Daylight dawns and it's time for the exam. Are we really prepared? Has all that cramming paid off? Or are we too tired to process the questions, much less remember the answers? We vow to never do this again to ourselves. We make a promise to God and try some bargaining. The next time, we say, we'll take the time to be better prepared. But please, Lord, help me just this once! Don't let me fail!

Jesus spoke a lot about cramming for finals and generally discouraged it. The story of the ten maidens in Matthew 25 is one case in point. The scene is a village wedding. The maidens are to be escorts for the bridegroom, carrying their lamps through the streets at the conclusion of the ceremony, headed for the marriage feast. The bridegroom is delayed, and all the maidens fall asleep, taking a well-deserved rest for what had been, for some, hours of preparation. The bridegroom comes. The maidens are awakened with a cry. "Come out to meet him! Bring your lamps!" Those who prepared in advance and filled their lamps with oil come out with joy and expectation. Those who failed to prepare are left alone to "cram for the finals." Five are forced to hunt for oil and ultimately are shut out of the marriage feast.

Cramming for finals is something we're all guilty of at one time or another, whether we're students in nursing or simply students of life. Time rolls on and work piles up. Our daily life of needed discipline gives way to functioning in a crisis mode.

The parable of the maidens, at first glance, seems a harsh one, a real guilt producer that would threaten to condemn us. But it's also a parable of hope. Jesus loves us enough to issue a warning for all the final exams in our lives, a warning to convict us, not condemn us. Prepare, he says. Make ready. Take time to reflect on what you really need to do in life to better prepare you for the tasks at hand, then do them. Then take time to rest in God's unfailing love and power to enable you to meet your final deadlines.

Lord, today as I reflect on all the upcoming "exams" in my own life and the various deadlines I must face, help me spend less time cramming for finals and more time slowing down and developing a disciplined walk with you.

God of the Valleys

> *And a man of God came near and said to the king of Israel, "Thus says the Lord, 'Because the Syrians have said, "The Lord is a god of the hills but he is not a god of the valleys," therefore I will give all this great multitude into your hand, and you shall know that I am the Lord.'"*
>
> 1 Kings 20:28

If you asked me what aspect of my job as a home-care nurse in upstate New York I most enjoyed, I would say it would be the valleys. Rural nursing is known for them. My daily trips to visit the elderly and homebound took me down many a dirt road, down into many a valley. The old abandoned barn I always passed on weekly visits to one of my clients, nestled in one valley among the hills, expressed my sentiments best: "God's Country," someone had painted on the side of the barn in bright, red letters.

Valleys, though, tend to have more negative connotations than positive. We talk about our spirits being down and sing about being down in the valley, the valley so low. We extend the image of a valley into the symptom of depression—a valley experience if ever there was one. Most of us, to be honest, would prefer to live in the hills and enjoy the life of a highlander. In the topography of hill country, life is more predictable, the long range view is better, you have perspective. Valleys aren't like that at all.

In our desire to be highlanders we have much in common with the Israelites. They, too, were considered inhabitants of hill country and usually descended to the valleys only reluctantly, and usually only for one purpose—to fight battles. The Amalekites and the Canaanites, archenemies of Israel, dwelt in the valleys (Numbers 14:25). Joshua fought his famous battle in the valley of Aijalon (Joshua 10:12). Countless other battles were fought, including battles against idolatry, in valleys. A final judgment of the nations will occur, writes the prophet Joel, in the Valley of Jehoshaphat (Joel 3:2). King David wrote a psalm about the valley experience, the valley of deep darkness, the valley of the shadow of death that he knew he would need to walk through in the future, even as he walked through many valleys of personal darkness in the present (Psalm 23).

"The Lord is a god of the hills but he is not a god of the valleys," the Syrians, also enemies of the Israelites, assumed. They didn't expect that God would help the Israelites fight in the lowlands. It wasn't their accustomed territory.

Yet God is there, in the valleys, if he is anywhere. David knew that. "Thou art with me," he proclaimed. God was with him in the valleys of his life, bringing direction, protection and comfort with his rod, his staff, his very presence (Psalm 23:4). God was with Joshua in the valley, causing the sun to stand still. God was with the Israelites in their various valley battles, scattering their enemies and bringing his chosen people through to victory when they placed their trust in him.

Today, Lord, as I drive through the valleys on my way to work, or walk through the valleys in my life, help me remember that this is, indeed, your country, too.

Empty Vessels

And Elisha said to her, "What shall I do for you? Tell me; what have you in the house?" And she said, "Your maid-servant has nothing in the house, except a jar of oil."

2 Kings 4:2

You're suddenly left alone to care for yourself and your children. Death of a spouse. Divorce. Desertion. The reasons vary for both women and men, but the end result is often the same. Your situation raises many questions. Who will provide for your needs? How will you meet your obligations?

In 2 Kings we have a situation not unlike the one many men and women face today, including many nurses who are faced with unstable employment situations and economic woes following a family crisis. There is no longer adequate financial provision for the family. The bill collector is at the door, beating it down, demanding payment. In the biblical story a widow is about to lose her two children, who are forced to become slaves or servants of the creditor to pay off the family debts. Then, it appears, a miracle occurs. Elisha tells her to borrow vessels from all her neighbors. Empty vessels. She is to fill these vessels with her oil, then sell the oil to pay her debts. She was able to pay off all her debt with just part of the olive oil. The oil, like the loaves and the fishes, appears to have multiplied.

A miracle. Elisha's ministry seemed to be characterized by them. He was often called upon to meet the needs of widows and orphans, and he did so in dramatic ways. Yet underlying this particular miracle of provision is another lesson—that of personal investment and personal responsibility to use the gifts or talents God has given us.

Reflect today on your own personal needs. Maybe, like the widow, they're financial. Perhaps they're related to a change in direction for your life, the search for a new job, the pursuit of a dream, the development of an avocation in addition to your vocation. Also reflect on your jar of olive oil. What does that represent for you? What are the gifts and talents God might want you to develop and use? And where are those empty vessels? What are you to pour those gifts and talents into?

As you reflect on an uncertain future, remind yourself to also reflect on your jar of oil. Ask God to show you the empty vessels that are waiting to be filled by someone like you, with your special gifts and talents, as you cooperate with God in your venture of faith.

Your Maker is Your Husband

> *For your Maker is your husband, the Lord of hosts is his name; and the Holy One of Israel is your Redeemer, the God of the whole earth he is called.*
>
> Isaiah 54:5

My husband died when I was twenty-five. I never remarried. We had no children."

"He's not my husband anymore since he developed Alzheimer's. Not in the physical and emotional sense, anyway."

"He'd been having an affair with his secretary for ten years. I never knew. And then he left me."

"When I developed multiple sclerosis my husband couldn't cope or wouldn't. He simply walked out the door and never looked back."

Death, disease, disability, and divorce. Recovering from the devastation of these four D's takes time. "It's rather like recovering from a hurricane," one home-care client said to me after the death of a spouse who had suffered both physically and mentally for several years.

Alone in a world where things don't make sense anymore —that's how these women felt. But they also shared a resource that made recovery from the storm possible. Not Ralph, or John or Ken or Steve. Not anymore. Not in the way they'd expected it would be. But the Lord, The Holy One, their Maker, promised to be like a husband to them.

"For the Lord has called you," continues Isaiah, "like a wife forsaken and grieved in spirit, like a wife of youth when she is cast off…. For a brief moment I forsook you, but with great compassion I will gather you" (Isaiah 54:6–7).

Nurses, too, often know the pain that comes from these four D's. Death, disease, disability, divorce. The prophet Isaiah has other words for us. We don't need to fear, we won't be ashamed, we won't be confounded. We can rest in God's everlasting love, knowing that any shame we've experienced in the past, any reproach, does not have to cling to us in the present or follow us into the future. For our Maker is our husband. He knows what we need, this Lord of Hosts. He takes the initiative to reach out to us in compassion, comforting us in our storm-tossed lives, helping us recover from the hurricanes.

The Last Leaf

He is like a tree planted by water, that sends out its roots by the stream, and does not fear when the heat comes, for its leaves remain green…

Jeremiah 17:8

If I were you, I wouldn't get old. I came from a family with nine brothers and sisters. Now I'm the only one left. The pain that's a lot worse than physical pain is the pain that comes when you're the last leaf on the tree."

Charles Murphy was telling me his story, warning me not to get old, warning me of the emotional pain that accompanied old age for him and, he reasoned, for anyone else unfortunate enough to outlive all their relatives.

The last leaf. Being the last leaf for Charles Murphy was a symbol of emotional pain and loneliness. He spent his days counting and recounting his losses, exhibiting little hope in the present or in the future.

The biblical writers were also well acquainted with the last leaves. For the prophets, last leaves often symbolized God's judgment. Like gardens without water, like oaks with withered leaves, are those who turn from the Lord, wrote Isaiah (Isaiah 1:30).

Yet as graphic as the image is of the fading, falling, shriveled last leaf, another picture emerges of leaves that are lasting: leaves that are used for healing (Ezekiel 47:12, Revelation 22:2), leaves that never wither, fall or die (Psalm, 1:3) but remain green (Jeremiah 17:8). What accounts for the contrast? The prophets and the Psalmist make it clear—trusting in the Lord and delighting in his Word. Blessed are those who trust in the Lord, whose trust *is* the Lord, wrote Jeremiah (Jeremiah 17:7).

When the heat comes, when the drought comes, when all the other leaves on all the other trees have withered and died, those leaves on other trees will continue to flourish and grow. Delight in the Word of God, meditate on it day and night, wrote the Psalmist (Psalm 1), and like a flowing stream that waters the roots of a tree that bears lush fruit and foliage, we, too, can water ourselves with the Word, then blossom and flourish, even to old age. That is a very special promise.

Being the last leaf on a family tree can be profoundly painful as we grieve our human losses, but it can also be an opportunity to share with others our wisdom and insight learned from many years of growing and a special ministry of prayer. That is a very special privilege.

Bedlam

"Return to your home, and declare how much God has done for you."

Luke 8:39

Bedlam. It's a place that was once described as an "insane asylum." Bedlam was not a place of healing but of punishment, where those with mental illness were crowded together, often restrained in chains and iron manacles in prison-like conditions. Care of the patient, wrote Josephine Dolan, a chronicler of nursing history, was purely custodial, with nursing attendants chosen not for their compassionate natures but for their physical strength.* Ironically, the actual historical Bedlam was originally Bethlehem Hospital, a hospice of St. Mary of Bethlehem. But the gentleness we associate with Mary, the mother of Jesus, was not a trait that characterized London's asylum for the mentally ill in thirteenth through eighteenth century England. An engraving of Bedlam by William Hogarth indicates that Bedlam was, in fact, a popular tourist attraction of London, with money from spectators used to help fund the hospital.

Bedlam. A place of noise or confusion. There was a place that must have seemed like Bedlam on the east side of the lake of Galilee. A naked man was living there, not in an asylum but in the tombs. Like the people of London's Bedlam, he, too, had been chained and fettered, but he'd broken the bonds that restrained him and fled into the desert, driven, Luke tells us, by a demon. In the last episode of the story, we see him sitting quietly at the feet of Jesus, bodily clothed and clothed in his right mind. In the postscript we see this same man begging Jesus to take him with him but becoming, instead, a missionary to his own people of Jesus' saving power and authority (Luke 8:26–39).

Fears of failure, feelings of inadequacy, histories of unresolved abuse, the inability to forgive, nagging guilt. Like the man in the tombs who was driven into the desert by the demon, we, too, as nurses, can be plagued by our own "demons": those issues that never seem to get resolved and that rise up to confuse us and cause us to be cast down or bound up. But Jesus would set us free, then send us out to tell others of his healing power and saving grace.

*Josephine A. Dolan. *Nursing in Society: A Historical Perspective.* (Saunders, 1973).

Light Bearers

Light Bearers

Her lamp does not go out at night.

Proverbs 31:18

She made her rounds at night, carrying a lamp. In 1857, Henry Wadsworth Longfellow immortalized her in a poem, "Santa Filomena." The Washington Cathedral, Washington, D.C., boasts stained-glass panels depicting various aspects of her life. Hundreds of biographies have been written for adults and also for children, featuring the lamp and the lady who carried it. There was a candle in the lamp, set in a candlestick, surrounded by a shield that kept it burning, protecting it from the wind.

Nurses are usually familiar with the image of Florence Nightingale carrying her lamp through the Barrack Hospital at Scutari, Turkey. The ward was larger than average; there were thousands of wounded and four miles of beds.

What did the lamp mean to those men? Stories abound, most of them probably fictional, but it isn't hard to imagine that one thing it probably did symbolize was hope. In that terrible, unbearable war with the horrible, deplorable conditions of those injured in battle, someone cared enough about those injured men to walk among them and shed some light, in the middle of the night. When they saw the lady with the lamp, the soldiers knew they were not forgotten. They knew they were not alone.

Lamps are meant to shine in dark places. The Barrack Hospital was a dark place, infested with rats, smelling of blood. Floors and men alike were caked in dirt. But a nurse with a lamp came into that dark place, bringing other nurses with her. They brought order out of chaos and a modicum of cleanliness from filth.

Lamps were also symbolically important to the Israelites. God, in fact, decreed that a lamp be kept burning continually, fueled by pure olive oil. In Exodus this light from the burning lamp was to be tended "from evening to morning" by Aaron and his sons, each of whom had a special calling to serve the Lord. They made certain the lamp did not go out at night. It was a symbol of the presence of God, continually dwelling in his tabernacle or tent of meeting (Exodus 27:20–21). In John's gospel, John the Baptist himself is described as a "burning and shining lamp" (John 5:35) who came to bear witness to the true Light of the world, Jesus Christ.

Lord, sometime today or this evening, I may be caring for the injured in body, mind and spirit. Remind me of my calling to be a light to those in the dark places of fear and pain, and help me to let them know that you dwell among them. Let me be a light and bear your light to those I'm called to serve.

I'm in Favor of That

> *For to us a child is born, to us a son is given; and the government will be upon his shoulder, and his name will be called "Wonderful Counselor, Mighty God, Everlasting Father, Prince of Peace."*
>
> Isaiah 9:6

It was Christmas on the Alzheimer's unit. I was working a double and doing the 5:00 P.M med pass. I was also passing out gifts to the residents—large print Christmas cards I'd made at home over the weekend that included various Scripture verses. My hope, for some of the more oriented, was that the cards might bring some light of recognition.

So far, they hadn't seemed to. George Stevens had grabbed one out of my hand and ripped it into shreds. Ralph Evans took his into the bathroom and flushed it down the toilet. Mary Roney proceeded to chew on hers. I was down to my last card and feeling less than hopeful.

"Merry Christmas," I said, handing Sophie Mitchell her medication and a glass of water. "I have something else for you, too, Sophie," I said, after she'd swallowed her pills.

Sophie took my card and turned it upside down. I turned it right side up. Then she began to read aloud the verses written on the card. She read hesitantly at first, then more clearly, but not, it seemed to me, with any sign of recognition of their meaning. But on my way out the door, Sophie brought me up short. "For to us a son is born," said Sophie. "I'm in favor of that."

It's been many years since I worked in Sophie's nursing home, and every year since I've attended a performance of Handel's *Messiah.* Handel was also familiar with the words of Isaiah, and even now, as I write this, I can hear the sopranos beginning to softly sing of the child that is born, the son that is given.

I remember the richness of the tenor and baritone voices that soon join the chorus to tell of the government that shall be upon his shoulder.

I am reminded again as I listen to the blending of the voices that this Son, this Child, is also called Wonderful Counselor, Mighty God, Everlasting Father.

And when the choir comes together in fortissimo to sing about the Prince of Peace, I also remember Sophie, and I echo her words in my heart as my own song of praise: "I'm in favor of that!"

Overflowing Hearts

> *My heart overflows with a goodly theme; I address my verses to the king; my tongue is like the pen of a ready scribe.*
>
> Psalm 45:1

A number of years ago I interviewed a retired missionary nurse. I asked her to reflect on what had given her life meaning and purpose over the years. One of the themes she kept coming back to was the meaningfulness of hymns.

Hymns, for Lily, brought back memories of times past with family and friends gathered around the piano. They were also vivid reminders of the faithfulness of God.

I asked her to tell me more specifically about hymns that triggered pleasant memories. The one that immediately came to her mind was "Fairest Lord Jesus." The picture that hymn triggered was of a young man plowing in a field adjacent to the spot her family had once stopped for a picnic lunch. "As he was plowing he was whistling that hymn," Lily said to me. "He probably had no idea what his whistling meant to strangers."

When the Psalmist's heart overflowed with a goodly theme, he turned his overflowing into hymns. Many of these, including Psalm 45, seem to be songs sung to a coming king, a longed-for Messiah. "You are the fairest of the sons of men" (v.2) sang the Psalmist. The writer of Lily's favorite hymn, penned in the late 1600's and whistled by the young farmer in the early 1900's, was surely inspired by that verse from the Psalmist written two or three thousand years ago. It is, we note, a love song to a king.

Lily went on to describe a hospitalization and a serious illness that nearly cost her life. The most meaningful aspect of that time for her was the remembrance of this hymn, this time not whistled but played on a tape recorder and placed on her bedside table by an anonymous nurse on a Sunday morning. "I don't remember anything else about my experience in intensive care," Lily recalled. "But I do remember that hymn and the other hymns reminding me of the resurrection and Jesus' power over all things, including me."

Incorporating the singing of hymns into our quiet times with God can be a way of expressing our own love for our Lord and King, Jesus. Most of them can also direct us back to Scripture for their inspiration, enriching both our time in meditation and our time of adoration.

We can also pray for opportunities to share hymns with others we care for as nurses, in the form of tapes or radios tuned to a station that plays hymns, or we can share with people in crisis entire hymnbooks, encouraging them to read the words of favorite hymns or even unfamiliar ones and turn them into prayers for whatever situation they are facing.

Lord, today may my own heart overflow with a goodly theme as I address my words to you in prayer and song. Let my tongue praise and adore you. Give me opportunities to share with those I care for the richness of some of these hymns of the faith to encourage their faltering hearts and flagging spirits.

Shirley, Goodness and Mercy

Surely goodness and mercy shall follow me all the days of my life; and I shall dwell in the house of the Lord for ever.

Psalm 23:6

It's very difficult for me to read the last verse of Psalm 23 without smiling and thinking of Christmas. The scene that comes to mind is a pageant at a local center in the area where I lived for developmentally disabled children and adults. Jim, the local chaplain, goes all out to make it a special time of celebration and involvement each year, even to the point of personally driving to a local petting zoo and transporting, in the back of his van, three live sheep for the pageantry. His tales about his adventures in animal husbandry are usually hilarious, and the three sheep have taken on personalities of their own. He's even named them—Shirley, Goodness and Mercy.

I could picture the pageant as he talked. By professional standards, it is nothing to write home about, but for the staff and relatives of the children, and for the children themselves, it's a highly professional production, on par with *Phantom of the Opera.* Two of the residents play the plum roles of Mary and Joseph. Three others play the wise men, filing down the aisle of the dining room-cum-stable, crowns askew and carrying, in varying assortments of pots from the kitchen, their homemade gifts of gold, frankincense and myrrh. Residential angels flap their handmade wings. And finally, in come the shepherds, running down the aisles, tripping over feet, smilingly confident they are being followed by Shirley, Goodness and Mercy.

David, the Psalmist-shepherd, also was smilingly confident, I think, that he was surely being followed, all the days of his life, by goodness and mercy. It was a clear and definite promise that he clung to, even in the midst of his present-day difficulties and future thoughts of death, just as surely as goodness and mercy were present that first Christmas morning when Jesus was born. The angel's message to the startled shepherds keeping watch over their flocks by night was surely one of goodness and mercy, telling of another Shepherd born who was "good news" coming into a "bad news" world and granting kindness in incredible excess of what could be expected. Good news of a great joy.

Jesus, I think, would be pleased at the pageantry displayed at the developmental center in his honor. There was pageantry, too, displayed in Bethlehem in the days surrounding his birth. There was a multitude of heavenly host praising in the heavens, wise men bearing gifts, and shepherds rushing "with haste" to see him, and, having seen, rushing out again to tell others.

Lord, today let me also run to you like the shepherds, smilingly confident that I'm surely followed by your goodness and mercy. Enable me to tell others the good news of your great joy—that we can dwell in your house forever.

Identification

And you know the way where I am going.

John 14:4

The evening shift in the nursing home or hospital has always been my favorite, not so much for the work itself but for the opportunities the work affords for giving spiritual care. Praying for those anticipating surgery or singing a hymn with them are expressions of spiritual care that individuals seem more open to. When the sun goes down they have more time to reflect and ponder on their situations. Spiritual care also can express itself through a hug or a hand on a shoulder as a physical reminder to a person in crisis that he or she is cared about in a personal way.

Spiritual care can also mean entering into the experiences of people who are lonely, afraid, in pain and in perplexity. The experience of "entering in" to meet spiritual needs is one of identification with what they might be experiencing, then help that enables them to reflect on their experiences in light of God's plan and purposes.

Scripture is filled with identification passages nurses can use to give spiritual care. These passages include stories of people who experienced many of the same situations people in crisis experience today: disease, disability, death and all types of other disasters that threaten life and limb. Identification passages also focus on feelings. Denial, anger, bargaining, depression and hope —all the stages of the crisis cycle are experienced by men and women of faith from Genesis to Revelation.

Consider the situation in John 14. The subject here is death. Jesus' death, to be sure, but also, in the future, the death of the disciples. They are anxious, troubled and confused about the future of the man they have come to know and love. They are questioning, doubting and perplexed about the nature of death, the existence of any afterlife and the way they're supposed to get there themselves. We can go to this passage ourselves as nurses and try and identify with the disciples, with their questions, their fears, their hopes. We can take our patients there, too, reading to them or loaning them a Bible.

Today as you spend time in John 14, pray for opportunities to share this identification passage with someone you care for, who may also be anxious and troubled and needs to know where he or she is going after death and the way to get there.

Sing Louder

> *...be filled with the Spirit, addressing one another in psalms and hymns and spiritual songs, singing and making melody to the Lord with all your heart...*
>
> Ephesians 5:18–19

Her evening routine was the same. Every night about eight, Maggie would come out of her room and walk down the hall, holding onto the railing. Nearly blind, she was still able to navigate the nursing-home corridors. She instinctively knew when it was time for a snack. By nine or nine-thirty I was usually finished with my med pass, and Maggie was finished with her crackers and tea. Then it was time for the walk back to her room. This time, though, Maggie always insisted on holding on to my hand, rather than the railing, and would tell me Bible stories on the trip back, reinterpreted a bit through the fog of her progressive dementia. Her favorite gospel, Maggie said, was "John the Baptist."

Maggie's favorite hymn was "What a Friend We Have in Jesus," but she made the hymn more personal by substituting *I* for *We*. Over and over she would sing, "What a friend I have in Jesus," rarely making it through the first verse.

"Sing with me," she'd insist, and, if I was hesitant or weak of voice, she'd squeeze my hand a bit and say to me, "Sing louder!"

Sing louder. Maggie's words of encouragement to shed my inhibitions apply to areas of life other than the nursing-home corridor. Maggie knew instinctively, I think, the best way to cope with times of fear, anxiety and depression, just as she knew instinctively what to do when you were hungry. What do you do? You sing. And when fears, anxieties and depression intensify, you sing louder.

Music and song, both instrumental and vocal, played a major role in the life of the early church. Israel's long history of journeying through the wilderness to the Promised Land was also marked by music. Not just quiet, instrumental after-dinner music, but praises rendered to God with the sound of the trumpet, the lute and the harp, the timbrel and dance, stringed instruments, organs and loud clashing cymbals (Psalm 150). And in the dark nights of the soul, both literally and figuratively, the Psalmist found that the Lord's song was with him and became, in fact, his prayer to "the God of my life" (Psalm 42:8).

This week if you're a little bit fearful, anxious or troubled of soul, take some time to sing to the Lord, like Maggie. If you're really fearful, anxious and depressed, also heed her wise advice. Sing louder!

Spirit Guides

> *Oh send out thy light and thy truth; let them lead me, let them bring me to thy holy hill and to thy dwelling!*
>
> Psalm 43:3

A number of years ago I came across a brochure advertising a continuing education offer for nurses. "Coming from New Zealand and Sedona, Arizona," read the announcement: "Energy Intensive Workshops!"

Workshop content, designed to foster spiritual development, included many things you didn't learn in Sunday school. Nurses would be taught how to channel past-life information, contact people who have passed over, exorcise entities, release trapped spirits and access information from their own and others' ascended masters and spirit guides. An evening celebration at the workshop offered a journey to the underworld. Workshop leaders included a native shaman and a healer who would use her channeling and intuitive skills to "bring out the best" in her students. The sponsor of the workshop was one of nursing's primary professional organizations.

In nursing we're faced today with a varied assortment of continuing education opportunities designed to appeal to our compassionate natures and desires to care for our patients and ourselves more wholistically. But not all nursing education is spiritually healthy, and some educational offerings, like the workshop in Arizona, can lead us into dangerous waters indeed. Discernment is needed to carefully evaluate both the practices taught in nursing and the theory behind those practices.

In the Bible God gives us some clear guidelines about discernment of spirits. For warnings about the dangers involved in channeling and contacting people who have passed over, see, for example, Deuteronomy 18:9–22 and Leviticus 19:31. The nations who were Israel's enemies gave heed to soothsayers, diviners and mediums; God did not allow his chosen people to do so. He did, in fact, call the practices abominable.

We are not, however, expected to go through life groping in the darkness. God has provided us with the ultimate spirit guide, the Holy Spirit, and the guidance of both the light and truth of the written Word that point us to Jesus, who has declared *himself* to be Light and Truth, to counter the counterfeit guides of the world. God's good guides are the ultimate rescue party for people lost and in need of direction.

The nursing continuing-education offering would have us travel on a journey to the underworld. The Psalmist's prayer was that God's light and truth would lead him to the holy hill of the Lord, directly to the Lord's dwelling and to God, his "exceeding joy" (v. 4). We are reminded in other passages that the Lord himself is our dwelling place (Deuteronomy 33:27; Psalm 90:1), our ultimate destination.

Channeling past-life information, contacting people who have passed over, journeys to the underworld: don't be deceived. The apostle John encourages us to test all spirits to see whether or not they are from God (1 John 4:1). The only true spirit guide will lead you to the Father, the Alpha and Omega of all life, and to the Son, Jesus Christ, the only true ascended Master. Jesus has not only come in the flesh, but has triumphed over death, giving us hope of eternal life. Now, that's my idea of a continuing-education offer!

Vision Required

> *And the Lord said to Paul one night in a vision, "Do not be afraid, but speak and do not be silent..."*
>
> Acts 18:9

Susan, a nurse who works on a labor and delivery unit in a large metropolitan hospital on the East Coast, was called into the administrator's office; a colleague had reported her for praying with a patient and questioned whether Susan could effectively care for people of faiths other than Christian.

A mandatory in-service for nurses on various alternative therapies with roots in occult philosophy was held in a small hospital in the Midwest. Mary and other Christian nurses in the hospital developed a packet of materials with information and requested a meeting with administration to discuss their concerns. The Christian nurses attended in-services where these alternatives were taught but did not participate in the practices, prompting colleagues to ask them questions about their faith. One nurse became a Christian because of their silent and verbal witness.

It's not always easy being a Christian in nursing. Meeting the spiritual needs of people in crisis can get you into trouble at times; refusing to participate in counterfeit forms of spirituality can, too. What do you need in order to stand up for what you believe is right in nursing? The encouragement of fellow Christians is one helpful thing. You also need a vision of what God wants you to do or say.

Visions, according to the dictionary definition, are something supposedly seen by other than normal sight—things perceived in dreams or trances or supernaturally revealed. They are generally thought to be special or out-of-the ordinary means of communication. From the perspective of Scripture, however, visions are not such out-of-the-ordinary occurrences. They were frequently the means by which God communicated his will and ways to people needing direction.

When Paul preached to the Jews in Corinth he met with much opposition. Uncomfortable with the negative response, Paul decided to stop witnessing to those of his own cultural persuasion and go, instead, to the Gentiles. God, however, had other plans for his reluctant servant. He reminded Paul, in a vision, of his presence with him, giving him words of encouragement. Paul had a job to do and the Lord made it clear he was not to be afraid but to speak out clearly for what he believed. Paul screwed up his courage and for the next eighteen months continued preaching the gospel. As a result, many Jews were saved. Paul was also brought up before the Roman tribunal on charges of violating the law by preaching the gospel; the end result of that encounter indicated Paul and his fellow Christians had nothing to fear from a "hostile administration" (Acts 18).

God may choose to give you a specific vision for what he would have you do in tough situations in nursing that involve taking a stand for what you believe. He has already given us many clear guidelines concerning many of those situations. The visions of Paul and of prophets like Isaiah or the ever reluctant Jonah (Jonah 1:1–3) are also vivid reminders to us of the claim God has on us as Christians to be bold in proclaiming our faith in word and in deed, trusting God to go before us and prepare the way.

Why?

Oh that you would keep silent, and it would be your wisdom!

Job 13:5

Why? Why did my baby die? Why does my husband have cancer? Mom's been such a good person; she served the Lord all her life. Why did she have this stroke? It's not fair!

Why is God silent?

The "why" questions, the "justice" questions: we hear them daily in nursing and often ask them ourselves. Occasionally legitimate reasons may surface, but for the most part, answers to these questions remain hidden within the realm of unanswered mysteries. Our role as nurses in helping people cope with suffering, their own or that of a loved one, really isn't to give answers, though, but to offer those who suffer our ears—the spiritual care intervention of two listening ears.

Job's friends are a good example of spiritual caregivers for the first seven days and nights of his suffering. Hearing "of all this evil that had come upon him, they came each from his own place, Eliphaz the Temanite, Bildad the Shuhite and Zophar the Naamathite." They came and they sat in silence, and "no one spoke a word to him, for they saw that his suffering was very great" (Job 2:11–13).

"In silence" is not always a comfortable place to sit. This becomes obvious as we see Job's friends' continued and clumsy efforts at spiritual caregiving and their unsolicited sermons of advice. As nurses, we too usually feel the need to do something or say something. We could offer the person good books on suffering, pray with them, read aloud some verses of Scripture or speak some words of comfort. And well we might, but silence is also "doing something" and, as Job reminds his friends, the very wisest thing we can do at times.

Job's primary need was for his three friends to be silent so he could speak to God himself, could argue his case and be heard. Job had a spiritual need to talk things out with God. God, if you're all-loving, why did you allow this to happen? God, if you're all-powerful, why couldn't you have prevented it? God, if you're all good, why do I feel so bad?

Lord, today in my nursing and in my own life, as I face suffering, help me to be more comfortable with the silences, seeing them as an opportunity to bring you my "why" questions and allow others to do the same, believing that you will speak in the silence, even if the only word I hear from you is "Trust."

On Call

On Call

Cast all your anxieties on him, for he cares about you.

1 Peter 5:7

My preference for nursing is long-term care. I like its predictability. I like to be in control, and long-term-care nursing meets my needs for stability and security. Time spent overseas as a short-term missionary, however, landed me in the role of an acute-care nurse, frequently responding to emergencies. I had been a nurse for two years when I found myself in Africa. It was a wonderful experience but also a bit scary. The most frightening time, for me, was the middle of the night when I was on call.

On those on-call nights I would find myself falling into a fitful sleep, ever alert to the Ethiopian equivalent to a paging system. My "pager" was not an operator sitting at a computer terminal but a little man in a long flowing robe who would come and tap very loudly on my window with his cane, summoning me to the hospital for an emergency. It was a pretty good system, if a bit unnerving.

I can still recall and relive the emotions I always experienced when I was awakened with the sound of the cane against my bedroom window. At first I was disoriented. That first month I remember leaping out of bed, unsure of where I was. Once oriented to my whereabouts, the usual feelings that flooded over me were those of anxiety. What was the emergency this time? A baby to be birthed? An accident victim? Would I be able to handle it?

The Lord, though, was gracious and reminded me (frequently) of his ability to help me cope and give me needed wisdom for the tasks at hand.

Many years later I was still an on-call nurse, only this time with a home-care agency in the United States. My pager was now a little black box with batteries that beeped very loudly in the middle of the night, alerting me to emergencies in the form of falls and fevers. Would I be able to cope with this particular emergency? Would I make the right decision? Should I go to that home in the middle of the night or is the problem something that can wait until morning?

Casting all my anxieties or cares for these people in crisis on the Lord became a habit. I had no choice. Though the context of Peter's admonition to the church in exile appears to be that of suffering and resisting temptation, I can also claim it for my own "sufferings through anxiety" and the temptation to think I can rely totally on my own strength and experience alone for any emergency situations. Peter's words remind me I also need God's wisdom and discernment for decision-making. I'm reminded, too, that after I have suffered anxiety for a little while, God will restore, establish and strengthen me for whatever job I'm called to do, when I'm on call. That is a very special promise.

Ministry of Memory

And the peace of God, which passes all understanding, will keep your hearts and your minds in Christ Jesus.

Philippians 4:7

For over ten years I cared for my mother as she became increasingly forgetful. A Christian for many years, she no longer began her day at the kitchen table, reading from her well-worn Bible. She no longer talked to me about God every night as she had done from the time I was old enough to remember.

Mom's days were filled with random words and unfinished sentences that seemed to mirror her inner state of disorganization. Her nights were filled with restless wanderings.

I would often read the Bible to her. She would sometimes fall asleep in her rocking chair or simply say to me, "That's enough of that," promptly get up in the middle of a familiar verse and wander off to putter in the kitchen or rummage in her bedroom drawers. At other times, though, there seemed to be a spark of recognition as she would repeat after me snatches of familiar passages and appear less anxious, less restless, more at peace.

I took her to church with me in the early years of care-giving, but we would rarely stay. Sometime after the opening hymn, and always before the sermon, she would turn to me and whisper in my ear, "I'm going," and off she would go, out of the pew, out through the door and back up the street to our home. As her disease progressed, however, church became a place of quiet rest. The hymns in particular seemed to have a calming effect, occasionally prompting my mother to sing a few familiar words herself, or to fall asleep, especially *during* the sermon, giving new meaning, said our pastor, to the concept of "resting in the Lord."

One night after I'd tucked her into bed, turned off the light, and reminded her that God and I both loved her, I asked her a question, not really expecting an answer. "Mom?" I asked. "Do you remember God?"

But she did answer unexpectedly, in the darkness of the room. "Vaguely," she said. "Vaguely."

The word *dementia* literally means "mind away" or "deprived of mind." As the disease process of Alzheimer's dementia scrambles the brain, many things are remembered vaguely, if at all.

In the New Testament Paul reminds the Philippians that as they rejoice, pray, praise and thank the Lord, God's peace that passes all understanding will keep their hearts and minds in Jesus Christ (Philippians 4:7). But how do people with dementia who are Christians do that? How can they continue to rejoice, pray, praise and thank the Lord when robbed of their very memory of Him?

I believe the answer is through other people as a ministry of memory. For our own loved ones and other people's loved ones we care for as nurses, ours can be a ministry of memory for them as we remind them over and over again of how much God loves them, of what Christ has done (and is still doing) for them, of whose they are and who they are in Christ.

We can do this by praying with them, by reading familiar passages of Scripture, even in the face of no visible emotional or verbal response. We can also bring them with us or arrange for them to go with others to places of worship and praise and community, to their home church or a hospital or nursing-home service—to peaceful places of collective memory where remembrances of God are shared, prayers are prayed, hymns are sung and rituals engaged in, and where hearts and minds, even those damaged by dementia, are kept in Christ Jesus.

Plain-Looking Women

> *...he had no form or comeliness that we should look at him, and no beauty that we should desire him.*
>
> Isaiah 53:2

No woman under thirty need apply to serve in government hospitals. All nurses are required to be plain-looking women. Their dresses must be brown or black, with no bows, no curls, no jewelry, and no hoopskirts." Dorothea Dix, a Superintendent in charge of Army nurses, shared this advertisement for volunteer nurses, circa 1860, and announced her requirements.*

Dorothea Dix, Sister Anthony of the Sisters of Charity, Linda Richards: these are the names of some of the women in nursing in the years surrounding the Civil War.

Dorothea Dix was in charge of volunteer nurses with a special concern for the mentally ill and with her own clearly delineated criteria for a nurse's resume.

Sister Anthony was one of those plain-looking women who fit Dorothea's job description. Age forty-seven and robed in a nun's floor-length habit, Sister Anthony pinned up her skirts so they "wouldn't drag on the deck" and set off on a riverboat for the Shiloh battlefields to care for the wounded.

Linda Richards came along a few years later, the first trained nurse in the United States, one of five students. No bows, no curls, no jewelry, no hoopskirts for her but active duty in a Boston hospital after graduation, every day from 5:00 AM until 9:00 PM and with nights on call for a dollar a week.

Sometimes I think nursing today is tough, but my nursing ancestors can always help me put the present in perspective. Many of them, historians tells us, were plain-looking women who surmounted many obstacles, including the ridicule and skepticism of physicians, to bear the burdens of others.

Nurses, like people in any profession, need role models to emulate. Role models give us vision, spur us on to the greater good, keep us humble and help us put our own lives in perspective. Dorothea Dix, Sister Anthony and Linda Richards are three of the best. But our greatest role model, and perhaps theirs too, is Jesus.

Jesus, Isaiah tells us, was not attractive or pleasant to look at either. He had no form or comeliness. From a human perspective there was no reason to esteem, desire or hire him. He was, in fact, despised and rejected by those he came to serve. The entire portrait Isaiah paints for us is that of a plain-looking man of no beauty, working endless hours on behalf of the afflicted and oppressed, caring for the wounded in body, soul and spirit.

Lord, give me your vision today of what it means to be a plain-looking man or woman in nursing, spurred on by that vision to seek the greater good of service in your name.

*M. Patricia Donahue. *Nursing, the Finest Art: An Illustrated History*. (C.V. Mosby Company, 1985).

Volunteers Needed

And I heard the voice of the Lord saying, "Whom shall I send, and who will go for us?" Then I said, "Here am I! Send me."

Isaiah 6:8

Nursing Volunteers Needed. All volunteer nurses will receive thirteen dollars a month. Interested women should report to their local hospital medical officials."

This newspaper ad, circa 1860, prompted a flood of responses from interested women, for a variety of reasons. For some, incredible as it may seem, it was the money. For others, war nursing meant escape from the monotonous routine of daily life. For others still, battlefields seemed as good a place as any to meet a future husband. But for others, answering an ad like the one above was like answering a call from God.

The history books tell us that not all nurses who volunteered stuck it out for the duration of the war. Unused to the stress and strain of battle and war hospitals, many nurses simply packed it in and went back home to a more secure environment. Food was scarce, you were surrounded by flying bullets, training was minimal and nursing the wounded was nothing their mothers had prepared them for.

So what made *you* decide to become a nurse? My own recollections center on an experience I had at age sixteen. I also answered an ad in our local newspaper, not for volunteers but for paid nursing assistants. For me, money was the motivator. I wanted to be an English teacher and needed to save for college. My plans soon changed.

Several weeks into the summer experience I found myself caring for a woman with dementia. For that one day this woman was my only patient. My task at the time was to keep her occupied and safe. Instead, she promptly ran away. I remember chasing after her around the hospital rose garden, pushing her wheelchair in front of me and praying I'd be able to catch her before she came to the river. When I finally got her back to her room, she crawled into bed and promptly went to sleep, appearing none the worse for her adventure.

I sat down in a chair beside her, sketched a picture of her sleeping, and wrote a letter home. "Mom," I wrote, "I want to become a nurse." As I look back now on that experience, I suspect that was my initial call from God, especially in light of what would become a nursing career caring for the elderly, in particular people with Alzheimer's disease, including my own mother.

Calls from God come to us at unexpected times in many forms. For some of us it's through experiences, for others it may be a still, small voice of inner knowing. God also guides and confirms through Scripture and the counsel of others. Some people, like Isaiah the prophet, have visions, coupled, perhaps, with a more audible voice asking, not demanding, that we volunteer.

Spend some time today reflecting on your own call to nursing. How did God direct and lead? When the going gets rough for you and the stresses and strains of nursing cause you to question your initial call and prompt you to second-guess your motives and decision, it will be important to remember that time you heard God ask you the same question he asked Isaiah. "Whom shall I send, and who will go for us?" Then you'll need to remember your response.

Rescue the Perishing

He has pity on the weak and the needy, and saves the lives of the needy.

Psalm 72:13

Telling people you are a parish nurse or trying to explain the concept is not always easy. Parish nursing may be interpreted as perish nursing. "Do you help people die?" one man asked me in my own church. My answer to him at the time was, "No, we try and help people live their lives more fully by getting them to pay attention to their health." But today as I read the newspaper, I'm reminded I really am in the business of perish nursing. All nurses who are Christians are.

"Rescue the Perishing, Care for the Dying" is an old hymn we used to sing in church, penned by prolific hymn writer Fanny Crosby. It's a hymn, I've noted, that's not in many hymnals today. I suspect the language Fanny used to describe people lost and in need of God has something to do with it. In our current culture, phrases like "snatching them in pity from sin and the grave" and doing it because "duty demands it" are met with a certain amount of skepticism. Pity? Isn't that notion obsolete? Doesn't it smack of superiority? Shouldn't we simply just empathize? And what about this snatching business? Isn't that a little heavy-handed? Then there's this line about our duty. I thought Christianity was a religion of grace, not works, but here I'm being told that duty demands I must save people. Don't I have a choice? Don't they?

The headlines in today's paper scream out at me about earthquakes on several continents, made all the more tragic by thousands of lives lost because of shoddy construction of buildings. On page 2 there's the story of a man who raped and murdered a child. On page 3 I read about a homeless woman who died on a city park bench, a rural farmer who committed suicide because of depression, a father and his four children killed in a hit-and-run accident in the suburbs. On page 4 I read about two high school students going on a shooting rampage, leaving dozens wounded in a church and several dead. On page 5 I read that the AIDS epidemic is decimating an entire country, leaving millions of children orphaned and victims themselves of the same disease. On page 6, abortions are up, hemlines are down.

Perish Nursing. Yes. We're focused in our jobs as parish nurses on prevention, but we're also in the business of death and dying as an inescapable calling. People around about us in the world are physically and spiritually dying each day. From the perspective of prayer, a missionary calling, an attitude of heart, our parish is the world. God so loved it, we are reminded in John 3:16; we must, too.

Lord, today as I go about the business of helping people locally live their lives more fully, don't let me neglect to pray more globally with a heart full of pity for the physical and spiritual needs of people in a world that needs rescuing and saving—by you.

Don't Neglect the Feet

The eye cannot say to the hand, "I have no need of you," nor again the head to the feet, "I have no need of you."

1 Corinthians 12:21

I was sixteen and a nurse's aide when I received my early training in patient care. We were taught that one of the most important parts of the human anatomy was the feet, and one of the most important aspects of a bed bath was to soak them. The title of the lecture was "Putting the Feet in the Basin."

Foot care is still important in nursing. Diabetics know this only too well. Feet must be washed and carefully dried to prevent skin breakdown. Nails must be carefully filed or meticulously clipped to prevent infection. Sadly, though, feet are a part of the anatomy that most often gets neglected for older people—personally, by relatives and even health-care workers. We simply don't know what to do with feet or, if we do, have little time to do it. I'd have trouble counting the times home care clients have asked me, "Please, do something with my feet." My inspections frequently indicated the need, not just for a wash or a soak or a good filing, but also for a good podiatrist.

The lack of good foot care has not always been such a problem. When guests come to call on us today, the first thing we generally do is offer them a cup of coffee or tea, but in biblical times, the offering was of a more personal, intimate and practical nature. Water was not just put on for coffee; it was also put out for feet. "Spend the night, and wash your feet," said Lot to the angels who came to visit (Gen. 19:2). "Wash your feet, and rest yourselves…" said Abraham to the three visitors who arrived at his tent door (Genesis 18:4). Abigail took time to wash the feet of King David's servants before going off to marry him (1 Sam. 25:41). Washing the feet of visitors was the expected thing to do.

The importance of foot washing continues as a theme throughout the New Testament. We see "a woman of the city, who was a sinner" washing the feet of Jesus with her tears, wiping his feet with her hair, anointing his feet with ointment and kissing them (Luke 7:36–38). We see Jesus carefully washing the feet of his disciples and wiping them with a towel (John 13:1–17). The mark of a true widow to be enrolled or entitled to help from the church was that she had "shown hospitality," "relieved the afflicted" and "washed the feet of the saints" (1 Timothy 5: 9–10).

Paul, too, uses the imagery of feet in 1 Corinthians 12 in his discussion of the diversity of gifts given by the Spirit to members of the church. "The eye cannot say to the hand, 'I have no need of you,' nor again the head to the feet, 'I have no need of you,'" said Paul to the Corinthians. From God's perspective and in his economy of things, all gifts and all people are of equal importance, especially, one might conclude, the not particularly attractive feet.

Lord, help me to be more aware today of those who may feel neglected, dispensable or unimportant, of people in need of "foot care." Show me what it means to "wash their feet."

We Wander a Lot

My sheep hear my voice, and I know them, and they follow me.

John 10:27

We started with some old favorites from large-print hymnals: "Amazing Grace," "What a Friend We Have in Jesus," "Rock of Ages." A few of the more oriented people in the group sang loudly. Some of the less oriented hummed. We said the Lord's Prayer together. Even those who rarely spoke, who couldn't remember who their loved ones were or even their own names, could remember the words to the hymns and the prayer. The importance of early rituals and well-formed habits in the lives of those with memory loss was always readily apparent on those Wednesday mornings in the Bible study I led at the nursing home in my role as a spiritual care nurse-coordinator. The URO group I called it: Ultimate Reality Orientation.

Now for the Bible study. Focus on the familiar. I read the Twenty-third Psalm out loud several times. Again, some of the residents joined me, repeating the words from the familiar King James Version.

Then I tried a question, hoping for some response but unsure of what to expect. "The Psalmist said the Lord is our shepherd. How are we like sheep?" I asked. There was silence. I asked the question again. Then one of the residents began to laugh and finally spoke. "We wander a lot," said Muriel.

As I look back on experiences I've had in nursing, caring for people with dementia, I'm always impressed with the good, sound theology that is frequently expressed. The symptom of wandering, so common to people diagnosed with Alzheimer's disease, is not just a symptom of dementia. We are all a wandering people.

People have wandered throughout biblical history. One generation of Israelites wandered in the wilderness for forty years as penalty for their disobedience (Numbers 32:13). They "wandered in desert wastes," wrote the Psalmist, before they cried out to the Lord who rescued them and "led them by a straight way" (Psalm 107:4–7). James encourages the early Christians not to wander from the truth (5:19). Peter wrote to the Christians in exile, reminding them that once they had wandered and strayed like lost sheep (1 Peter 2:25).

Jesus also was well aware of our propensity to wander and of the need to be brought back to the truth of the gospel. "As he went ashore he saw a great throng, and he had compassion on them, because they were like sheep without a shepherd; and he began to teach them many things," we read in Mark's Gospel (Mark 6:34).

For sheep, the solution to wandering has always been the same; they need to get to know their shepherd. Jesus makes it clear that those who hear and know their own shepherd's voice will follow him alone and not be led astray by any stranger. Those who hear and know their shepherd won't wander from the sheepfold.

Lord, I know that I, too, like Muriel, am prone to wander. Let me instead get more intimately acquainted with you, that I may hear your voice clearly calling me to follow you and you alone in the midst of all the other voices clamoring for my attention.

Wakefulness

> *And the Lord came and stood forth, calling as at other times, "Samuel! Samuel!" And Samuel said, "Speak, for thy servant hears."*
>
> 1 Samuel 3:10

Wakeful. I need to be wakeful. If you've ever worked the night shift in a retirement home you know how hard it is to be wakeful, especially around four in the morning. A foggy haze sets in, and you're grateful to the client who rings his call bell to give you something to do that involves physical exercise and takes you away from the pile of paperwork on the desk. Or maybe you're a student studying for a final exam and need a dose of wakefulness. Or perhaps you're a nurse involved with research and working under the pressure of deadlines for a grant proposal that's due, all in the wee hours of the morning. You, too, know you need to be wakeful.

Alert, watchful, vigilant, expectant. Wakefulness is a quality many nurses need and need to cultivate. It's also, I think, a spiritual need we all have.

Consider Samuel. He was just a young boy, but already he had a pretty responsible job, "ministering to the Lord" under the direction and tutelage of a priest named Eli. As I read his story I'm struck by one phrase, the same one used to describe Jesus. Samuel "continued to grow both in stature and in favor with the Lord and with men" (1 Samuel 2:26).

How did Samuel do that? By being in a state of wakefulness. In the early morning hours, just before the dawn, we know he's in the temple lying down but in a state of wakefulness. When the word of the Lord does come to him he doesn't hesitate; he runs, even though he's yet to truly know the One who called him. Samuel is wakeful, alert, watchful, vigilant, expectant. Speak, Lord, for thy servant has ears to hear, says Samuel, and God does speak to him and to others through him, letting "none of his words fall to the ground" (1 Samuel 3:19).

Lord, teach me what it means to be in a state of wakefulness, ever vigilant and listening for your word. Like Samuel, enable me to hear and know your voice calling me to obedience and to the study of your Word. Cause me to grow in stature and in favor with you and with those you put in my path to serve.

A Future and a Hope

> *For I know the plans I have for you, says the Lord, plans for welfare and not for evil, to give you a future and a hope.*
>
> Jeremiah 29:11

Recently a friend who was in charge of an orthopedic nursing unit told me she went to work in the morning, only to discover the unit itself had disappeared over the weekend. Patients were shuffled to other parts of the hospital, and the unit she was in charge of was closed. She still had a job, but she was counting the days, she said, until her "pink slip" came.

I once worked for a health agency that changed its name four times in the year I was working there as the company was bought and sold in the face of economic crisis. Cutbacks. In cities across the United States and Canada, nurses are experiencing lay-offs as health-care facilities close their doors, downsize or merge.

How do you cope with the crisis and uncertainty of change and job insecurity? For some nurses, change is a challenge and losing a job simply launches a search for another. "Life is an adventure," a friend of mine describes her own situation. But for most of us, the possibility of unemployment is a fear to face. When we are certain God called us to a job in the first place, then are suddenly confronted with the loss of it, fears intensify, coupled with doubts about our own ability to hear God's voice.

What does God say to us in the midst of impending job loss or the uncertainty of change in any aspect of our lives? Trust in him and his good plans for our future. "For I know the plans I have for you, says the Lord, plans for welfare and not for evil, to give you a future and a hope." Instead of trusting God, I have a tendency to trust in the circumstances. When those circumstances differ from my vision and my version of what should be happening, it's easier to panic than to trust.

In the third year of the reign of Jehoiakim, king of Judah, King Nebuchadnezzar came to Jerusalem and besieged it, taking the people of Judah captive, carting them off to Babylon. Talk about changed circumstances and pink slips! Yet in the midst of their forced exile, God reminded them not to fret. "For I know the plans I have made for you," said God. Their deliverance might not happen immediately, but God would be faithful to fulfill his promise to them; they could count on it.

In the meantime they were to live and work as if they were to be in that exiled place forever. "Build houses and live in them; plant gardens and eat their produce. Take wives and have sons and daughters; take wives for your sons, and give your daughters in marriage, that they may bear sons and daughters; multiply there, and do not decrease" (Jeremiah 29:4–6). They were called to work diligently and to "seek the welfare of the city" where they had been taken into exile and to pray for the city, the place of their employment, "for in its welfare you will find your welfare," said the Lord (Jeremiah 29:7).

No matter how precarious our work situations or how badly we might want to be employed somewhere else, God's call to us is clear. Bloom where we're planted. If we do that and listen for his voice, he will take care of our future.

Weary of
Well-Doing

Weary of Well-Doing

Brethren, do not be weary in well-doing.

2 Thessalonians 3:13

I'm weary," my friend Dorothy told me on the phone. "I'm weary *of* well-doing."

I wasn't surprised. She'd just come off a weekend on call, describing it as "the worst one I've ever had."

The hours had been long, including a phone call at 4:00 A.M. to restart an infusion on an ill home-care client in need of antibiotics. "Every time I thought I'd seen my last client and I was home for good, my beeper would go off or the phone would ring and off I'd go again. Please pray for my weariness."

We did pray together on the phone. Dorothy prayed especially to be reminded that God did not grow weary and she'd experience some of his strength to get her through the rest of the week. I prayed for my own weariness in the midst of moving, too many teaching responsibilities and the telltale signs of a cold coming on. We also prayed for each other.

Weary *of* well-doing was not exactly how Paul, Silvanus and Timothy phrased it in their letter to the Thessalonians, but I think they knew what we both meant and felt. Dorothy's personal application and paraphrase of 2 Thessalonians 3:13 certainly seemed valid. Weary *of* well-doing is the way we home-care nurses get sometimes when the beeper goes off at two in the morning, we just got in from a prior call an hour earlier and know we have many a client to see before the weekend is over. The Thessalonians also, I think, were weary *of* well-doing in addition to being weary in it.

The church in Thessalonica was a young church but a relatively healthy church. The Christians there were facing some opposition and some, Paul says, were "living in idleness, mere busybodies, not doing any work" (2 Thessalonians 3:11). The majority who were working diligently needed to be reminded to stand firm and not give up or cave in to external pressures or the call to slack off and just get by. Paul, Silvanus and Timothy had even boasted to others of the steadfastness of the Thessalonians' faith in spite of persecutions and in the midst of afflictions they were enduring. Though their situation was different with respect to their specific difficulties and reasons for their weariness, their basic need was the same as Christian nurses on call: to be strengthened in the steadfastness of Christ and to continue in the love of God.

This week if you get weary *in* well-doing and *of* well-doing, find a friend and pray together. Ask the Lord to give you his strength in your weariness, his compassion in your tiredness, his "peace at all times in all ways" (v. 16). And keep on keeping on.

Sacrifice of Praise

> *Through him then let us continually offer up a sacrifice of praise to God, that is, the fruit of lips that acknowledge his name.*

Hebrews 13:15

Anne, a nurse from Canada, sent me an e-mail recently. "Yesterday," Anne wrote, "I was at the hairdresser's, and she told me about a dream she had. We were praying together in the dream, and I said in the dream, 'What I really need you to pray about for me is sacrifice.'"

The hairdresser's comment to Anne in the dream was, "We bring a sacrifice of praise."

"This has prompted me," wrote Anne, "to do a study on sacrifice. I think God may be telling me to be more bold in proclaiming with my lips the glory of his name."

Sacrifice and praise: these two concepts seem to be at cross-purposes to each other. The notion of sacrifice for most of us conjures up visions of want, giving up and denial of creature comforts. Praise, on the other hand, is generally associated with plenty, gifts received and blessings bestowed. Yet God tells us these concepts are intimately related.

I think of David in Psalm 22, a good Psalm to help us re-orient our understanding of prayers in times of trouble. "My God, my God, why hast thou forsaken me? Why art thou so far from helping me, from the words of my groaning? O my God, I cry by day, but thou dost not answer; and by night, but find no rest," David complains. But then he abruptly changes his focus. "Yet thou art holy, enthroned on the praises of Israel. In thee our fathers trusted; they trusted, and thou didst deliver them. To thee they cried, and were saved; in thee they trusted, and were not disappointed." (vv. 1–5).

God, the Scriptures tell us, inhabits the very praises of his people. This is something I often forget when I'm in my own troubling situations and crying out for help. The words of my own groaning and cries of my heart sometimes get so loud I'm unable to hear God's still, small voice telling my soul to be quiet, to praise, to trust.

The Psalmists did complain and groan and cry aloud a lot, but they also praised a lot. They praised in the morning (Psalm 5:3) and at night (Psalm 119:62); they praised with the lyre and harp (Psalm 33:2); they praised God in the good times and bad (Psalm 34:1). And they called all creation to join them in the chorus—angels and hosts, sun, moon and stars, fire and hail, snow and frost, beasts of the field, birds of the air and all creeping things, the rich and the poor, the old and the young (Psalm 148). No one and no aspect of God's creation should be exempt from lifting God up, enthroning him with praise.

Why is praise so intimately associated with sacrifice? I think it's because for most of us, praising when we haven't yet experienced answers to our prayers is a difficult thing. It seems counterintuitive. Yet it is often in praise, rather than mere petition, that we see God act, because praise is a reminder to us not of what God can do but of what God has done. We know we can trust him for our future because he has proved himself to be trustworthy in our past.

I'm grateful for my friend's reminder to bring my sacrifice of praise to God and not just my petitions. Thank you, my friend, for sharing with me what God has been teaching you this week.

Putting Out to Sea

And embarking in a ship...we put to sea...

Acts 27:2

I once had a friend who had been in the same job for twenty-five years. That kind of commitment is commendable for most people but not, I would have to conclude, for my friend. Every year for many years she would call me at some point to complain about her job. She considered it a "dead-end street," a "job where I'm not learning new skills," a place where "I feel stifled."

Every year I would listen patiently to my friend's litany of complaints, and then I would tell her the same thing. Change jobs!

Her response was always the same. "Well, maybe. I'll think about it. Changing jobs is scary." She thought, but never made the move.

Why do we stay in jobs that we consider dead-end streets and places where we feel stifled? Sometimes it may be because that's where God has called us; we're to bloom where we're planted and pray for a change in attitude and perspective. At other times, though, it may be related to our personal fears and anxieties and not the will of God.

The disciples and apostles had fears and anxieties, too, in relation to their ever-changing job descriptions, but also, I think, a sense of adventure. One phrase repeated over and over in both the Gospels and the book of Acts in reference to Christ's followers is, "we put to sea." They always seemed to be getting in and out of boats. They were never totally sure of their destination and frequently faced both "gentle" and "tempestuous" winds but they kept moving forward, headed for the other shore.

Sometimes when they set sail they were simply sensitive to the Spirit guiding and directing after spending time in prayer. Sometimes the choice was made by others. When Paul put out to sea with fellow Christians Luke and Aristarchus, headed in the general direction of Italy, it was not a trip he made voluntarily but was a forced exile. They sailed in many ships in between Jerusalem and Rome and came into many ports of call. They found themselves coasting along "with difficulty" (Acts 27:8). Then there was a shipwreck.

But through it all they survived, others were saved and healed and the Christians continued to have a sense of adventure and anticipation of what God might do through them to reach others with the good news of the gospel.

Today, if you feel you're in a dead-end job and find yourself complaining, ask God to show you if you're to bloom where you're planted or if, instead, you're to hoist your sail and set out for other shores.

Hallelujah!

Hallelujah! For the Lord our God the Almighty reigns.

Revelation 19:6.

The day began at 6:00 A.M. with a blood draw for a fasting blood sugar. Then there was a quick ride off to the lab across the city to deliver it and then on to thirteen other home-care clients with a varying assortment of needs, primarily wounds that required dressing changes. Many of my home-care clients that Sunday in December were burn victims, requiring multiple dressings on arms and legs and abdomens. My total dressing count was mounting up. By noon I figured I'd changed a total of twenty dressings and had six more people to see.

Lunch was nonexistent, and dinner consisted of a chicken-salad sandwich quickly eaten in my car. *Weary* was the operative word. Four hours later I pulled into the driveway of my last client, an elderly man with glaucoma and diabetes who lived alone and needed nursing help to put in his eyedrops and administer his insulin. Sitting in the driveway following the visit, I breathed a huge sigh of relief and turned on the car radio. The music was highly appropriate. I headed for home, turned up the volume and sang along to the welcoming strains of the "Hallelujah Chorus."

God, I thought, has an incredible sense of timing and knows what I need to lift my spirits and put my work in perspective.

The "Hallelujah Chorus" is probably the most familiar and beloved of all the choruses from the *Messiah*. Reflecting on it that December night, though, I was struck with another of its attributes. Handel didn't place it at the beginning or at the end of his oratorio, but somewhere in the middle. There's still, he reminds us, much work to be done, but we can take time out in the midst of the daily busyness to pause and remember that God reigns.

The "Hallelujah Chorus," like all the other choruses in Handel's *Messiah*, is meant, I believe, to lead us back to Scripture. In this particular chorus I am reminded not only that the Lord reigns but that the kingdom of this world has become the kingdom of Jesus. I may not always be aware of it in the visible sense, but I know in my heart it is true. God is at work behind the scenes of the visible in spite of diseases like diabetes and glaucoma or the terrible accidents associated with fires. God is in the business and the busyness of healing, using nurses in the process to stabilize the blood levels, alleviate eye pain and bind up the wounds of the afflicted.

Lord, today let your kingdom be made more visible to others as I communicate your care for them in my nursing. Let it be more visible to me in the business and busyness of my days and nights. Help me, too, in my own weariness, to pause and remember that you reign and to sing with the choir, Hallelujah!

The Easy Yoke

> *Take my yoke upon you, and learn from me; for I am gentle and lowly in heart, and you will find rest for your souls. For my yoke is easy, and my burden is light.*
>
> Matthew 11:29–30

When I was a new graduate and nurses still wore caps, I had attached a tiny gold pin in the form of a yoke to one corner of my cap, over the purple ribbon. Another friend in nursing had given me that pin for a graduation gift. Because it was unique, not the cross many nurses wore on their caps or the more traditional-looking class pin on the uniform, patients and family members would often ask me what it meant. It gave me the opportunity to share with them the biblical significance of being yoked with Christ in my nursing.

I think I have a clearer sense today about what that truly means, after dozens of years of nursing, than I did as a new graduate fresh out of college. So do some of my friends.

"Take my yoke upon you," said Jesus, "and learn from me; for I am gentle and lowly in heart, and you will find rest for your souls." These words of Jesus were directed to people who were weary and heavy-laden, weighed down, perhaps, by heavy physical work loads or emotional and spiritual stress. Jesus seems to be speaking most personally to his disciples. Like nurses, they also knew about heavy laboring and long workdays. Hanging around with Jesus ensured that. The picture Matthew initially paints for us is one of burden, like that of an animal harnessed and pulling a plow or oxen pulling a cart.

How can pulling a plow or drawing an oxcart with a yoke around your neck be an image of rest? Other biblical references to yokes represent anything but rest, figuratively conjuring up images of political slavery to foreign kings (Deuteronomy 28:48) or even bondage to sin (Lamentations 1:14). At first glance it might seem as if being yoked represents a mighty heavy burden.

In the literal sense, however, a yoke is a wooden bar or frame used to join two animals, which enables them to pull a heavy load by easing the pain of the pull. This yoke is symbolic of a union. The yoking of the two doesn't eliminate the burden, but it makes the burden borne much lighter.

This is what Jesus is saying to me. I don't have to pull that cart alone. Jesus is next to me, teaching me how, giving me lessons on burden bearing. Gentle and lowly: these are the words he speaks to describe himself. Easy and light: these are the words he speaks to describe the pulling of the heavy load, as long as I'm yoked with him.

For It Is in Giving

There came a woman of Samaria to draw water. Jesus said to her, "Give me a drink."

John 4:7

How many of you here are the oldest child?" This question was asked at three different nurses' conferences I attended. In response to the question, two-thirds of the audience stood up or raised their hands. Implied in the question and in the response was a belief that oldest children had a tendency to become caregivers, especially caregiving nurses. Only children do too. Nearly half the nurses in each audience were also caregivers of aging relatives.

There is one problem with the word *caregiver.* Implied in the word is the notion that the person who is a caregiver gives but does not receive. From a biblical perspective, nothing should be further from the truth. The words in the poem by St. Francis of Assisi, "For it is in giving that we receive," remind us of this, as does the life of Jesus. Jesus, in his interactions with others, gave and received freely. It was, in fact, often in his ability to receive that his greatest caregiving was shown to others.

Jesus requested a drink of water from the woman of Samaria (John 4) to quench his human thirst. In doing that, he broke the cultural boundaries of race (A Jew requesting something of or even talking to a Samaritan), gender (a man considered a rabbi or teacher talking to a woman) and social prejudice (a man considered a holy man or great teacher talking to a woman considered a prostitute). He offered her, in turn, eternal life. Both the physical needs of Jesus and the spiritual and emotional needs of the woman were met in the exchange.

Jesus also readily received the ministrations of a woman in the house of Simon (Luke 7:36–50). She anointed his head with costly fragrant ointment and washed his feet with her tears. In turn he gave her the highest of compliments and affirmations. Her story will be remembered and her name will be recorded in history for her caregiving sacrifice of a "beautiful thing."

Jesus expressed his delight in Mary, who sat at his feet and listened to his teaching, honoring him with her attentiveness (Luke 10:38–42). Jesus received from her an open ear; in turn he offered his wisdom.

"For it is in giving that we receive," wrote St. Francis. Jesus said it too. "Give and it will be given to you; good measure, pressed down, shaken together, running over, will be put into your lap. For the measure you give will be the measure you get back" (Luke 6:38). The thought expressed is not that we give in order to receive, but that in our giving we will receive, we can count on it. And as the stories of Jesus and the women illustrate, it is also in receiving that we give some of the greatest gifts to others, including the gift of a renewed self-esteem.

Turn and Change

Put away the foreign gods that are among you, and purify yourselves, and change your garments…

Genesis 35:2

At least every two hours from 11:00 P.M. to 7:00 A.M., residents in nursing homes are assisted to turn over in bed, and linen is inspected for incontinence. We even have a phrase that's used routinely for this anticipated activity for nursing assistants working the night shift—turn and change. Turn and change. Turn and change. In the middle of the night, for the nursing assistants, this phrase becomes their mantra as they walk from room to room, pushing a linen cart down the hall, going into rooms and turning and changing people.

Turning and changing older people in nursing homes, afflicted with diseases like arthritis or Alzheimer's, is not always an easy task. Those with stiff arthritic joints may cry out in pain, and those with cognitive impairment often resist all attempts to be turned. Scratches and bruises are not uncommon occurrences on the night shift, as nursing assistants fall victim to flailing arms and legs of resistive residents who simply want to be left alone, not changed, not turned. But who could blame them? Painful for some, at the very least it disturbs one's sleep.

Yet research shows that turning and changing is good for you. Good for circulation. Good to prevent skin breakdown. Good to prevent contractures if arms and legs are massaged and repositioned.

I can identify with those resistive residents. Turning and being changed is something I'd rather not do. Change is something I often resist. It hurts. It's painful. I like my old routines. Bad habits are especially hard to change and be turned from.

I'm "accustomed to do evil" as Jeremiah reminds me, rather than doing good (Jeremiah 13:23). I need to turn and be changed.

God was always telling people to turn and change. Sometimes they listened, sometimes they didn't. "Put away the foreign gods that are among you, and purify yourselves, and change your garments," Jacob says to his household and all that were with him (Genesis 35:2). If they wanted to make the trip to Bethel, they first needed to turn and be changed.

Lord, help me today to turn from those things that are stumbling blocks in my relationship with you and turn, instead, toward you. I want to be willing to turn and change and be turned and changed by your Spirit, working in my life.

The Flashlight

Thy word is a lamp to my feet and a light to my path.

Psalm 119:105

I made my way slowly up the stairs, inching my way through the darkness, holding on to the rickety railing. Finally a sliver of light appeared from under the door at the top of the stairs. I knocked and the door was thrown open by Ralph.

"Hi, yah," he said.

"Hi, yah." I replied. "What happened to the light?"

"Oh, that's just George again," Ralph replied. "When he gets mad he unscrews the lightbulb."

I was making my weekly community health visit to a family in the inner city. Ralph was the eight-year-old son of Myrtle. Myrtle was my client. Myrtle needed dressing changes for an abdominal-wound infection and also needed some health teaching concerning her new infant, born two months premature. Even with the light bulb screwed in, the stairs were pretty precarious, but this was ridiculous. George was the landlord. We needed to have a talk.

I remember the phone conversation later that day with an irate George and his reluctant promise to keep the bulbs screwed in. Usually he did, but not always, so for the next month of evening visits I carried a very large flashlight in addition to my routine nursing paraphernalia. The week before Christmas I carried two; one was a gift for Ralph. I also gave him a children's Bible. "He does love to read," his mother told me once.

The last visit I had to that family was, in fact, on Christmas. I still remember the warmth of their tiny kitchen and the smell of Myrtle's stew. It reminded me of the stable. Four-legged creatures abounded—a dog, three cats, a mouse I detected scurrying behind the stove, a veritable army of cockroaches that defied all attempts to do them in by any means. The baby, now quite healthy, slept in his mother's arms, swaddled securely in a blanket. And Ralph, the "man of the house" as he called himself, and the only one I had ever seen *in* the house, sat on the living room sofa, reading his new Bible in the dark by the light of his Christmas flashlight.

"Thy word is a lamp to my feet and a light to my path." the Psalmist wrote. Working in the inner city, I often found myself holding on to many a rickety railing and climbing many a staircase with inadequate lighting leading up to tiny apartments like Myrtle's and Ralph's, people who were poor by middle-class standards and could use a little light in their lives to alleviate their material poverty, but who were often, I thought, far richer in spirit than the rest of us.

I don't know whether Ralph continued to read the Bible after Christmas, but I hope and pray he did. I am thankful to him for also reminding me to live less by sight, more by faith, more by the light of God's Word.

Someone to Worship

So he argued in the synagogue with the Jews and the devout persons, and in the marketplace every day with those who chanced to be there.

Acts 17:17

Chapter 17 of Acts tells the story of the apostle Paul's attempt to convince the people in Athens that they could possess spiritual well-being by putting their faith in a personal God instead of in impersonal idols and the one "unknown" god they had been worshipping.

Paul begins his discussion of the nature of God by noting that the Athenians were a very religious people, possessed, it seemed of an innate spirituality that created a desire to worship someone or something. Athens at that time was a metropolis famous for its various statues and temples to a wide assortment of deities, including the goddess Athena, who was considered the patron of arts and wisdom. Also living in Athens at that time were philosophers from various schools of thought—the Epicureans and the Stoics.

The Epicureans believed that gods existed but these gods did not intervene in the affairs of men. The primary practical goal of Epicureanism was that of achieving happiness or well-being (and avoiding pain) by serene detachment.

The Stoic school of philosophers was also dominant in Athens. The Stoics believed that Reason was the source of life in the universe and the means by which men should live. Happiness or well-being for the Stoic was found in the self and was independent of the external world of other persons and things. Overcoming passion and emotions versus detachment from them was a goal of Stoicism.

Into this eclectic melting pot of beliefs, Paul introduced another conceptualization of reality, that is, the notion of one personal, knowable God, separate and distinct from the universe, who created all people, made in the very image of himself. Paul's understanding of the meaning of spirituality was that all people were created for the express purpose of having a personal, intimate relationship with their creator. The Christian hope, says Paul, is that all people might "seek God," "feel after him" and "find him" (v. 27). He says this is possible because God is totally unlike the deities they have been worshipping, either as "unknown" or as "homemade," but is a personal God who came to earth in the flesh, in the person of Jesus Christ.

True spiritual well-being, Paul believed and taught, came from believing in both a wholly Other yet a uniquely personal God and what this God had done for human beings through Jesus; repentance rather than reason or escape from reason was the chief requirement for salvation and happiness.

Unlike the gods or non-gods the people in Athens had been worshipping, the God Paul spoke of was a God who could actually meet their needs because he was totally self-sufficient and respected people as whole people with physical needs, emotional desires and spiritual longings. There was no need to suppress or deny the self by retreating *from* the world, because the God Paul offered them was a God who would show them how to live in relation *to* the world.

Lord, help me to learn how to argue and reason in the everyday marketplace of my nursing world, with my colleagues who have different world views and with others who chance to be there, that you are a personal God.

Amazing Grace

Amazing Grace

O come, let us sing to the Lord; let us make a joyful noise to the rock of our salvation!

Psalm 95:1

When I first met Maggie [whom you met in "Sing Louder"], she was sitting on a table in the third-floor dining room of the nursing home where I worked. I was just coming back after a two-week vacation, and there were a number of new residents.

"Who's that?" I asked Doris, one of the nursing assistants.

"Oh, that's just Maggie. She always sits on the table, or under it."

When I came into the dining room later for the 7:00 P.M. med pass, Maggie was sitting, legs crossed, leaning against one of the table legs, her arms raised above her, her body swaying back and forth as if in a trance.

"Maggie, what are you doing under the table?" I asked.

In response to my question, Maggie began to sing. Softly at first and then more loudly. The words to Maggie's song were a little mixed up but the tune was familiar: "Amazing Grace." Doris, the nurse's aide, laughed. "She thinks she's at camp meeting. That table is her tent. She does this every night, and if we try to get her out, she screams and hits us. So we just let her get it out of her system until she tires out."

Maggie, I later discovered, had grown up in South Carolina and was a nurse herself. "Going to camp meeting," where enthusiastic hymns were sung and fiery sermons preached, was a way of life for her. This way of life, we soon discovered, Maggie planned to continue in the nursing home. Diagnosed with dementia, Maggie was not very oriented to twentieth-century realities of time, place and person but her mind was still filled with concrete memories of her growing-up years and experiences with God.

Maggie also suffered from the respiratory distress of chronic obstructive pulmonary lung disease and required regular doses of inhalers to enable her to breathe freely. My task as evening charge nurse was to ensure that Maggie did inhale every two hours, not an easy one given Maggie's predilection for "camping out." But I finally came up with a solution; I crawled under the table with Maggie, who was "happy," she said, "I'd come to call." So we sang "Amazing Grace" together, pausing between verses for Maggie to puff on her inhaler, while all around our table, nursing assistants and some of the residents and visitors clapped and also sang along.

The Psalm writers are constantly encouraging us to sing to the Lord, to make a joyful noise. We are to come into his very presence with thanksgiving, to worship and bow down, to kneel before him. When I think of my own response to God, it often lacks the expressiveness and fervor encouraged in the Psalms. Maggie reminds me of my need for that. Totally uninhibited, Maggie freely praised the Lord in her own constructed "tent of meeting" and insisted others join her. I often think, as I look back on this and other experiences I had with Maggie, that it was she, and not the rest of us, who was really oriented to the only true and ultimate Reality.

Lord, today let me be as uninhibited as Maggie. Let me come to you with arms outstretched, responding with my prayers and songs to your amazing grace.

Longing for Love

...you are precious in my eyes, and honored, and I love you…

Isaiah 43:4

I was looking for some historical references on nursing in my local library for an article I was writing on Florence Nightingale. Instead I discovered the following books: *Nurse Donna's Dilemma*, *Nurse Vicky's Desire*, *Nursing in the Caribbean*, *Nurse Susan Awakens*, *The Nurse and the Handsome Stranger*, *Circus Nurse*, *A Lover for Nurse Hudson.*

Then there were the associated on-line book blurbs. In *Longing for Romance*, Millicent McCarthy, only recently recovered from a breakdown following the death of her fiancé in an auto crash, takes a position as a nurse on a country estate in England and falls in love with a man who has amnesia. In *Long Lonely Nights*, a nurse from rural Connecticut relocates to New Orleans during the Mardi Gras and finds dangerous love and romance in the Louisiana Bayou.

Florence and some of the other historical figures who rose to prominence in nursing history got short shrift on the library bookshelves compared to fictional characters like Nurse Donna, Nurse Vicky, and Millicent McCarthy. Adventures in the Crimea couldn't compare to intrigue in the Louisiana Bayou.

Romance novels are all the rage today, including novels that include nurses as heroines. You see them everywhere, including locker and employee break rooms in hospitals and nursing homes and even on tables in nurses' stations.

So what is their appeal? Well, sex is obviously one, and adventure tinged with danger. But going deeper, the appeal is to the heart, to longings for fulfillment and the need for intimacy. Most of us, if we're honest, want lives with happy endings, a bit of adventure along the way to keep life interesting, and a partner sensitive to our needs who will love us passionately.

The good news is, the offer of all three is readily available, and all between the covers of some books with considerably longer shelf lives than that of *Longing for Romance.* There's the book by Luke with the happy ending, characters returning to their city with great joy. For adventure there's the book of Acts. It's filled with heroes who survive shipwrecks, false imprisonment and falls off horses. Daniel, too, is great suspense. Will the characters survive the fiery furnace? Who will rescue them from the lions' den? Will the king recover from his madness? You can't beat Esther either for intrigue. What a heroine!

If a sensitive lover is what you're looking for, check out Ruth, and consider her suitor Boaz. Think about the prophet's response to his unfaithful wife, Gomer, in Hosea. Read the Song of Solomon and blush. Go to Isaiah to hear about the God who loves you with an everlasting love, speaks tenderly to you, calls you precious in his eyes and honored. I love you, says this God. You are mine.

Wow! Talk about romance!

Lord, help me when I'm longing for romance to bypass the Bayou and come directly to the source. And thank you for including me in the script of the greatest romance novel ever written: yours.

Feasting on the Word

> *Thy words were found, and I ate them, and thy words became to me a joy and the delight my heart; for I am called by thy name, O Lord, God of hosts.*

Jeremiah 15:16

Many years ago I attended a conference on counseling. I was working at the time with student nurses on college campuses. One assignment was to bring a written case study of a particularly difficult situation we were facing. We were to meet with a counselor during the week to discuss our case.

For most of us, myself included, the "case" turned out to be "us." I was the person in need of counsel. I still remember being on my knees before the Lord and experiencing the most profound sense of forgiveness. It rivaled my experience of salvation many years earlier. I was simply overwhelmed with the love of God as the counselor pronounced words of forgiveness, grace and mercy.

I went back to my room after my experience, opened my Bible and began to read. I remember the verse well from Jeremiah, the prophet, who mourned and wept: "Thy words were found, and I ate them, and thy words became to me a joy and the delight my heart; for I am called by thy name, O Lord, God of hosts." Jeremiah, too, knew what it meant to experience forgiveness, grace and mercy.

Eating the words of God. Feasting upon them. Joy! Delight! The rejoicing of the heart. Jeremiah tells me I am called by the name of the Lord, precious in his sight, loved and forgiven.

The context of Jeremiah is one of a people in exile, surrounded by enemies—persecutors, the wicked, the ruthless. Yet it is in that context that God brings the message of hope. He will deliver. He will forgive and restore those who turn to him in repentance.

What do you need to hear from God today? Whatever it is you will find it in his Word. Ask him to give you today a desire to feast on his Word and the words you need to feed on, words of joy and delight that can remind you of who you are and whose you are.

Bearing Our Burdens

Bear one another's burdens, and so fulfill the law of Christ.

Galatians 6:2

Who is the nurse's nurse? Who lends you a hand, a listening ear, a word of encouragement when the going gets rough? Who is your visible means of support? Who helps you carry your burdens, or, more literally, shoulder your boulders, in your times of greatest need?

What should you look for in other people that could meet the criteria for an adequate personal support system? Who affirms, applauds and acknowledges your abilities, personally and professionally? Who accepts you, just as you are, faults and all, but also encourages you to change and grow, offering you constructive criticism and helping you objectively evaluate your strengths and weaknesses? Who calls you lovingly to accountability? Who can you be really real with? Who can you laugh with and cry with? Who's sensitive to your unspoken thoughts, feelings and desires? Who do you just enjoy being with? Who just enjoys being with you? Who can you go to for help at any time, day or night?

No one person can meet all the support needs we have. We need to cultivate a variety of personal and professional relationships even as we build into the lives of others by affirming, applauding, accepting, acknowledging them and calling them to accountability. Raising questions about our support system may also stir up within us deep longings for deeper degrees of intimacy with friends and relations. They do in me as I reflect on my own relationship needs and my own abilities and shortcomings as I strive to be a better friend to others.

We were created to live in relationship. Throughout biblical history we see examples of close relationships among friends, relatives and neighbors. David and Jonathan, Ruth and Naomi, Paul and Timothy and the people described in the New Testament church who sold all their possessions to live and support each other in community are all examples of close relationships.

One other relational model we have of a supportive relationship is Jesus with his disciples. What Jesus was to his close friends and companions, he can also be to us.

Jesus wants to affirm us, applaud us and acknowledge our abilities. He also accepts us, just as we are, faults and all, yet encourages us to change and grow, offering constructive criticism and helping us objectively evaluate our strengths and weaknesses. He calls us lovingly to accountability and wants us to be really real with him, bringing to him our laughter and our tears. He's extremely sensitive, too, to our unspoken thoughts, feelings and desires and longs for us to enjoy being with him even as he enjoys being with us. And he's available, any time, day or night. What a friend!

Today take time to reflect not only on your own interpersonal needs for a support system, thanking God for friends who love you, but reflect, too, on your relationship with Jesus as your ultimate supporter, who will help you bear the burdens and shoulder the boulders in your personal life and work in nursing.

A New Name

> *...and you shall be called by a new name which the mouth of the Lord will give. You shall be a crown of beauty in the hand of the Lord, and a royal diadem in the hand of your God.*
>
> Isaiah 62:2–3

"I Will Change Your Name." I remember the first time I heard that song, written by D.J. Butler. The seminar speaker had been teaching on the topic of shame and disappointment. She called us to reflect on the names we call ourselves that define our identity, often in negative ways: "wounded," "outcast," "lonely," "afraid." These are the same names D.J. Butler chose to identify in his song. There are others, often associated with shameful events in our past that continue to haunt us, and names others have given us as "labels" that still stick to us. I clearly remember those from grade school associated with my surname, Fish. I was not amused!

People we care for in nursing may also define themselves by names: "anxious," "troubled," "fearful," "unable to cope," "chronically or terminally ill," "noncompliant or difficult."

Names have always been important to God and the people of God. The Bible gives us a glimpse of their rich history and importance. Over eleven hundred times the word *name* occurs, highlighting the importance of individual identities of people and places. Children are named by parents with names that reflect the circumstance of their births and the longings of their heart. In her dying moments, Rachel gives birth to *Benoni*, the "son of her sorrow," who is also named *Benjamin* by his father, meaning "son of my right hand" (Genesis 35:18). Hannah's newborn is named *Samuel*, meaning "heard by God" (1 Samuel 1:20).

Names are remembered and people are honored and chosen, by God, by name, for special tasks, at special times, in special places. "I know you by name," God says to Moses, immediately before revealing himself and his own name to Moses as his gracious and merciful Lord (Exodus 33:17–23). Twelve precious stones, each symbolizing the name of one of the Israelite tribes, were attached to a pouch and worn "upon the heart" of the high priest, a symbol of the value and worth of God's people, whom he chose, by name (Exodus 28:15–30). And lest we should doubt his attention to detail and individual identity, the Psalmist reminds us that even the stars are numbered and named by God (Psalm 147:4; Isaiah 40:26).

But names are also changed. God named and renamed. *Abram*, which means "exalted father," became *Abraham*, "father to the multitude" (Genesis 17:5). *Jacob* becomes *Israel*, "he who strives with God" (Genesis 32:28). The unstable Simon, Son of John, was called Peter by Jesus, a name that means "rock" (Matthew 16:18). Jerusalem, the once faithful city that had "become a harlot," would be called faithful again, and "the city of righteousness" Isaiah 1: 21–26).

"Confidence," "joyfulness," "overcoming one," "faithfulness," "friend of God," "one who seeks my face": these are the new names God gives to the wounded, outcast, lonely and afraid in D.J. Butler's song. "A crown of beauty" and "a royal diadem": these are the new names God gives to the forsaken and the desolate needing a new name in Isaiah.

Lord, today as I reflect on those names I have called myself or others have called me that have put me to shame, free me from names that prevent me from living my life in joyful confidence with you. Let me see myself today as you see me, as a crown of beauty, your royal diadem, precious in your sight. Show me how to communicate your love to anyone else who crosses my path today who needs a name change, that they might find their true identity in you.

Searching for the Sheep

> *For thus says the Lord God: Behold, I, I myself will search for my sheep, and will seek them out.*
>
> Ezekiel 34:11

In *Nursing, The Finest Art: An Illustrated History*,* M. Patricia Donahue estimates that between two thousand to ten thousand women were engaged in nursing and hospital administration during the Civil War. While statistics vary greatly, depending on one's source of information, one vital fact that all historians agree on is the important role Mary Ann Bickerdyke, a widow with two young children, played in that war. Mother Bickerdyke was the name the soldiers called her. Her own personal call to nursing appeared to come from God, delivered in a plea by her pastor, Henry Ward Beecher, urging women of his congregation to volunteer for service on the battlefields of war.

Florence Nightingale had a window named after her, but Mary had a ship. In 1943, the hospital ship, *S.S. Mary A. Bickerdyke* was launched in Richmond, California.

Donahue notes that Mary Ann Bickerdyke was involved in many activities, including the organization of kitchens, hospital laundries and even an ambulance service. But the activity she engaged in that is most remembered by historians was her midnight ventures to the battlefields, searching for injured soldiers who might still be alive and in need of nursing care. To read the accounts of her exploits is to read of a nineteenth-century Mother Teresa, caring for those on whom others had given up, then fighting for their rights and needs. An untitled and unsigned woodcut of the era shows Mary castigating a surgeon for neglecting the soldiers; care and treatment in the military camps, according to newspaper accounts, was sadly lacking.

Ezekiel paints a graphic picture not unlike the scenes of Civil War battle, the back-streets of Calcutta or other places in the world today where the sick and suffering are neglected, including North America. "My sheep were scattered," says God through the prophet, "they wandered over all the mountains and on every high hill; my sheep were scattered over all the face of the earth, with none to search or seek for them" (Ezekiel 34:6). Ezekiel vividly describes the weak who need strengthening, the sick who need healing, the crippled who need binding up, the strayed who need to be brought back to the fold and shepherds who have neglected them all, looking only to their own needs and interests.

God himself, Ezekiel says, will rescue his sheep, will bring them out and gather them from the far places, will feed them on the mountains and by the fountains, will be, in fact, their shepherd, seeking the lost, bringing back the strayed, binding up the crippled, strengthening the weak and feeding them all in justice (vv. 11–16).

Today as you pray, remember women like Mother Bickerdyke, Mother Teresa and countless other missionary-minded nurses who have answered a call to minister to those neglected by societies with little concern for justice. There may also be people abandoned and neglected today in places where you work in nursing—the unborn, the homeless, the abused. Pray Christian nurses would be faithful to hear and answer the call to care in special places of darkness.

*M. Patricia Donahue. *Nursing, the Finest Art: An Illustrated History.* (C.V. Mosby Company, 1985), pp. 285–300.

I Love You

> *...but the Lord your God turned the curse into a blessing for you, because the Lord your God loved you.*
>
> Deuteronomy 23:5

Wednesday mornings at the supermarket. My mother loved the outings, but as her dementia progressed, it became more difficult to take her shopping. She had a habit of sitting down when she was tired, and sometimes that was in the middle of the floor. I finally bought a wheelchair that was very portable. I'd push Mom's wheelchair in front of me and pull a cart behind me, up and down the super market aisles.

The lines were long that morning. The check-out clerk was new, slow, making mistakes. The people in front of us were not patient. You know the type. They glare. They swear. Finally it was our turn. Then my mother said it. "I love you." The clerk looked up. My mother said it again. The clerk started to cry. Then she wiped away her tears and finished processing our order, smiled at my mother and said, "Thank you."

I love you. My mother rarely spoke, and when she did the speech was usually disconnected and garbled, but the phrase "I love you" was one she often did say, and clearly. She said it to everybody. She'd said it to her doctor just the week before, prompting him to blush! To me it seemed quite natural that Mom would simply say, "I love you," to this clerk.

What did this clerk need? A shorter check-out line, for one thing, and a few less ornery shoppers, to be sure. But the primary thing she needed was the reassurance that no matter how many mistakes she made, someone still loved and accepted her, just as she was, faults and all.

I love you. I think of the countless times I've been in the position of that checkout clerk—in a new job where I felt over my head, not meeting the expectations of others or myself. How good it was to remember or be reminded in those times that I was loved, not necessarily by my immediate supervisor and not for my productivity on the job, but loved and accepted by my Father, who ultimately employs us all.

I love you. I also think of the times when I've grown impatient with check-out clerks, with family members, friends, colleagues, and with my own employees when I was director of a health-care agency. What if, instead of "glaring and swearing" when people aren't meeting our expectations, we simply said to them, "I love you"?

Deuteronomy 23:3–8 tells the story of the Ammonites and the Moabites who actually hired someone to curse Israel. The Lord turned that curse into a blessing— because God loved his people. God can turn the curses against us into blessings; what's meant for us as "evil" God can turn into good, not because we deserve it, but simply because he loves us.

Lord, show me ways today I can communicate to others, in my nursing and in my home, your very special message to those who need it: I love you.

Have You Heard About the Waterfall?

And how are they to believe in him of whom they have never heard? And how are they to hear without a preacher?

Romans 10:14

We walked for about a half hour, then went back to Margaret's house for dinner. "Have you heard about the waterfall?" she asked me.

I had heard of it but hadn't a clue as to where it was. Since my recent move to Canada to teach Parish Nursing, a number of people had mentioned it to me, and one of these days I knew I wanted to find it.

"Well you don't have to go very far," Margaret said. "It's about two miles from where you live."

The next morning I took off, armed with directions from Margaret. As I rounded the bend on Waterdown Road, I saw a small dirt trail winding down into a valley. I stopped, got out of my car and heard a gentle roaring. A few feet from the road, but well hidden from view, was a waterfall, tucked behind the trees, with the sun dancing like diamonds on the rocks as the water cascaded into the valley.

"The voice of the Lord is upon the waters," sang David in Psalm 29:3. I suspect he might have composed some of his psalms next to a waterfall like mine. The spot near the trail soon became another home away from home, a place of quiet and rest. A place to pray and read the Bible or a book, "far from the madding crowd"* as the saying goes, with the background music of the waterfall, the voice of the Lord on the waters.

One morning I was reading Romans, sitting by my waterfall. "And how are they to believe in him of whom they have never heard?" wrote Paul. "And how are they to hear without a preacher?" I needed a preacher to find this particular spot on the trail. My friend Margaret befriended me, walked with me, invited me for dinner, told me about this wonderful, peaceful place that is my idea of a little slice of heaven on earth. I doubt that I would have found it on my own, even with a map, given my poor sense of direction. I needed more than a map. I needed someone to point the way, tell me how to get there.

Lord, there are so many people who would love this waterfall if they only had someone to tell them about it. And it's really very simple when you think about it. All you have to do is invite someone to walk with you, then, while you're sharing a meal, ask them a simple question, "Have you heard about the waterfall?"

*Novel title by Thomas Hardy, *Far From the Madding Crowd*, 1874, based on a quote from the poem, *Elegy Written in a Country Churchyard* by Thomas Gray, 1751.

Gentle Among You

> *But we were gentle among you, like a nurse taking care of her children.*
>
> 1 Thessalonians 2:7

What does biblical history say to us about nursing? Plenty, beginning in the Old Testament, and it's really an exciting read.

Consider Rebekah's unnamed "private-duty" nurse in Genesis 24:59. She traveled with her reasonably well-off employer (by camel vs. cruise ship), to meet Rebekah's future husband Isaac; she presumably stayed employed when Rebekah married, helping care for little Jacob and Esau, who undoubtedly gave them all considerable headaches.

Some biblical "nurses" were a lot like us; they also complained about overwork. Consider Moses. In Numbers we find him voicing concerns about his job description. "Why hast thou dealt ill with thy servant? And why have I not found favor in thy sight, that thou dost lay the burden of all this people upon me?" Moses says to God. "Did I conceive all this people? Did I bring them forth, that thou shouldst say to me, 'Carry them in your bosom, as a nurse carries the sucking child, to the land which thou didst swear to give to their fathers'?" (Numbers 11:11–12). Had there been unions in those days, Moses might have been the first to sign up!

Other biblical images of a nurse are less fractious. Many depict women literally nursing and caring for infants. Consider Naomi, the mother-in-law of Ruth; she took Ruth's newborn, who was to become the grandfather of King David, and "laid him in her bosom, and became his nurse" (Ruth 4:16). Rescued by Pharaoh's daughter, Moses was cared for by his nursing mother. The qualities associated with these and other Hebrew women who were nurses were concern as they rendered care and nurturance as they offered nourishment.

Also consider God himself, who is likened to a father nursing or "bearing his son" (Deuteronomy 1:31). Paul alludes to this same image in Acts 13:18, speaking in the synagogue about the God who "bore with them," caring for them in the wilderness for forty years. A parent nursing an infant is the image Paul meant to convey. The metaphor extends from one of caring for an infant to one of carrying an older child in his arms. Isaiah 60:4 paints a beautiful picture of a nursing God carrying. "Your sons shall come from far, and your daughters shall be carried in the arms" says Isaiah to an Israel in exile. The actual image is that of a father nursing or safely carrying an infant out of captivity to a place of peace and security.

Consider Paul and the apostles. Paul tells us more about the qualities of a good nurse; *gentle* is his operative word. "Like a nurse taking care of her children" is how the gospel is to be communicated—with gentleness and a sharing, not just of words, but "also our own selves," writes Paul (1 Thessalonians 2:7–8).

Nursing, the scriptures remind us, is caring *for* the whole person *with* our whole persons. What a legacy we have; what a privilege is ours.

RESOURCES FOR NURSES

Nurses Christian Fellowship (NCF) is a professional and ministry organization that encourages nursing students and graduate nurses to meet for Bible study, prayer and fellowship. NCF offers professional membership, in-person and online conferences and webinars, Bible studies and other helpful resources, and nursing continuing professional development. NCF USA is a ministry of InterVarsity Christian Fellowship (IVCF).

For NCF USA contact:

Nurses Christian Fellowship
P.O. Box 7895
Madison, WI 53707-7895
e-mail: NCFmailbox@intervarsity.org
https://ncf-jcn.org

For NCF Canada contact:

Nurses Christian Fellowship Canada
38 Clydesdale Rd
Markham, ON L3R 3S9
e-mail: nationalchair@ncfcanada.ca
https://ncfcanada.ca

NCF USA and NCF Canada are member countries of Nurses Christian Fellowship International (NCFI): https://ncfi.org

Journal of Christian Nursing (*JCN*) is a peer-reviewed, quarterly publication of Nurses Christian Fellowship, USA. The mission of *JCN* is to help students, nurses and nursing educators practice from a biblically-based, Christian perspective. Nursing continuing professional development contact hours are available in each issue. JCN is a benefit of professional membership in NCF USA. For order information and submission guidelines see:

https://journals.lww.com/journalofchristiannursing/pages/default.aspx

Books for Nurses and Nursing Schools on Spiritual Care

Called to Care: A Christian Vision for Nursing. (Third Edition, 2021). Judith Allen Shelly (RN, BSN, DMin), Arlene B. Miller (RN, PhD), and Kimberly H. Fenstermacher (RN, PhD, CRNP). IVP Academic.

Nursing as Ministry. (First Edition, 2021). Kristen L. Mauk (RN, PhD, DNP, CRRN, GCNS-BC, GNP-BC, FAAN) and Mary E. Hobus (RN, MS, PhD). Jones and Bartlett Learning.

Spirituality in Nursing: Standing on Holy Ground. (Seventh Edition, 2022). Mary Elizabeth O'Brien (RN, PhD, MSW, MTS, FAAN). Jones and Bartlett Learning.

About the Author

Sharon Fish Mooney is a registered nurse. Her PhD in nursing is from the University of Rochester. She has worked in nursing homes as a staff nurse, nursing supervisor and spiritual care coordinator, was director of a home care agency in rural upstate New York and was a staff worker with Nurses Christian Fellowship. She spent a summer as a missionary nurse in Ethiopia with the Sudan Interior Mission and taught Parish Nursing and spirituality courses at McMaster Divinity College, Hamilton, Ontario, Canada. She currently teaches nursing research and other courses online for Regis University and Indiana Wesleyan University. She cared for her mother with Alzheimer's disease for over ten years and has published a book and articles on caring for a loved one with dementia. She is also a published poet and translator of French poetry. She lives in Ohio with her husband, Scott.

www.ingramcontent.com/pod-product-compliance
Lightning Source LLC
LaVergne TN
LVHW050630100826
845148LV00011B/1816

* 9 7 9 8 3 8 5 2 7 7 7 5 9 *